GET REA

What course participants are saying. . .

*"**Get Real!** prophetically carries the heart of God to His people, Participating in the course has meant that my life in Christ will never be the same again."*

"The taster day did not prepare me for the total brilliance of the course."

*"The **Get Real!** teaching has been the most challenging I have encountered in 20 years of Christian living."*

*"I can pray for people for hours in meetings, but I can't love them for ten seconds. That's why **Get Real!** is important."*

*"I wanted to stop reacting to circumstances and instead start responding to God. **Get Real!** taught me how."*

"There was a genuine affection for one another in the group with times of laughter and tears as we opened our lives up to each other."

"What a rich experience it has been – real food for my soul."

"The course is so powerful. It is the gospel of Christ made practical."

"Great multi-sensory teaching. Personal testimony was particularly moving and meaningful."

*"**Get Real!** isn't touchy-feely, lovey-dovey psychobabble. It's very practical, and it's helping me accomplish the most important things a disciple can do."*

GET REAL!

Walking in the light towards true relationship
Pursuing God's design for community

Roselyn Abbott

First published by Matteh Publications,
Central Hall, St Mary Street, Southampton SO14 1NF.

ISBN 0-9545535-0-0

British Library Cataloguing Data
A catalogue record for this book is available
from the British Library.

Book design and production for the publishers by
Gazelle Creative Productions Ltd,
Concorde House, Grenville Place, Mill Hill, London NW7 3SA.

*'Who is this coming up from the desert
leaning on her lover?'*

Song of Songs 8:5

For Richard

CONTENTS

ACKNOWLEDGEMENTS

I hope that *Get Real!* will encourage you to love God as He is and to love others as He has loved you. Many of the concepts in this book have been drawn from the foundational work of Larry Crabb, Selwyn Hughes, Leanne Payne, Mary Pytches and Windy Dryden. The escalator example in chapter 4 has been adapted from something similar in *Preparing for Client Change in Rational Emotive Behaviour Therapy* by Windy Dryden. Likewise the ABC theory of emotion was originally expounded and popularised in secular psychology by Albert Ellis, among others. The text has been illustrated by the skilful hand of Jackie Morgan. Allan Cox, Clare Suffield, Angie Barr, Norma Parrack and Dot Palmer-Fry have each contributed significantly to *Get Real!* through their encouragement and support. Thank you to all these people. I am in your debt.

As the Christian discipleship course *Get Real!* has become established, I have found myself part of three very different families: my nearest and dearest at home, and the team members of both *Get Real!* and Central Counselling and Training Service, Southampton. In these three families I have been really loved. A few more corners of my soul have rubbed off and a little more of me has become real. Thank you for really loving me: husband, children, friends, prayer warriors, colleagues, teammates, *Get Real!* participants and counselling clients alike. Thank you for being God's *message*.

FOREWORD

Hundreds of years ago, in the fourth century AD, a famous Christian preacher and teacher by the name of Augustine said, 'Salvation is God's way of making us real people.' Roselyn Abbott, in this book *Get Real!*, takes things a stage further and shows us *how*.

There is just no escaping reality. Millions of people attempt to do so every day but it is a pointless exercise. At the start of every road we think will lead us away from facing what is real, there is a sign that reads, 'No Way Through'. One of the sad things about this generation is that, though it brags about its realism, it is a generation that has invented more ways of escape than any other.

Professionals who work in the field of mental health tell us that our mental and emotional well-being can be measured by how willing and able we are to face reality. Roselyn has done us all a great service by putting a clear focus on the issue of what it means to be a real person and showing us the steps we need to take in order to live a life of reality.

For that reason I regard the issues discussed in this book as of immense importance. Indeed, it would be difficult to think of a subject that has more importance. Yet it is all so understandable, so readable, so applicable. As I read through the book I found myself mirrored again and again in Roselyn's insightful writing.

I am struck also by the warmth of this book. It is one thing to communicate insight; it is another thing to do it with warmth. Although there are many challenges in these pages, I find in the crafting of every chapter a generous spirit at work and thus the whole book speaks with compassion to where we all live and move and have our being.

I think you, as a reader of this book, will be gratified for the time invested. Enjoy the feast that lies ahead of you!

Selwyn Hughes

CHAPTER 1
WHY GET REAL?

Discipleship is about becoming. It is a life-long learning and doing process. For my own reasons, and without necessarily realizing it, I have chosen a unique road on which to travel through my life, my own particular way of becoming. I am the disciple of whatever I unconsciously or consciously use as my blueprint. Somehow I determine to set myself apart from other ways of being in order to become like that which I believe will provide me with a better existence. I always have faith in someone or something. It is just what it means to be human.

Maybe my heroes have been folk who achieve through hard effort. Somewhere along the line, I have learnt that working hard is the way to ensure an adequate and even a satisfying existence. Without realising it, I find myself becoming something of a workaholic. It is the road I travel, as I become a disciple of work. Maybe you admired folk who are gentle and unassuming and so you learnt that reticence could ensure that you enjoy a pleasant life and even reliable safety in relationships. Without realising it, you find yourself becoming something of a wallflower.

In Christian terms discipleship, or becoming, is learning to 'walk the talk' of salvation. My task is to so admire my selfless hero Jesus Christ in His modelling of perfect humanity that I become like Him: *'I want to know Christ and the power of his resurrection and the fellowship of sharing in his sufferings, becoming like him in his death and so, somehow, to attain to the resurrection from the dead'* (Phil 3:10).

Becoming like Him in His death. This is the bottom line of Christian discipleship – to become a living demonstration of Jesus in His absolutely selfless love for others. As I read those words of the apostle Paul and attempt to make them my own, I flinch at the thought of having the same attitude as Christ, a willingness to really suffer, lose out and even die for the well-being of another. I also have no idea how to put this selflessness into practice in any of my relationships.

Outside Scripture, I think that the process of Christian discipleship is perhaps most eloquently and simply described in the powerful children's classic *The Velveteen Rabbit*:

'What is REAL?' asked the Rabbit one day...' Does it mean having things that buzz inside you and a stick-out handle?'

'Real isn't how you are made,' said the Skin Horse. 'It's a thing that happens to you. When a child loves you for a long, long time, not just to play with, but REALLY loves you, then you become Real.'

'Does it hurt?' asked the Rabbit?

'Sometimes,' said the Skin Horse, for he was always truthful. 'When you are Real you don't mind being hurt.'

'Does it happen all at once, like being wound up,' he asked, 'or bit by bit?'

'It doesn't happen all at once,' said the Skin Horse. 'You become. It takes a long time. That's why it doesn't often happen to people who break easily or have sharp edges, or who have to be carefully kept. Generally, by the time you are Real, most of your hair has been loved off, and your eyes drop out and you get loose in the joints and very shabby. But these things don't matter at all, because once you are Real you can't be ugly, except to people who don't understand.'

'I suppose you are Real?' said the Rabbit...

'The Boy's Uncle made me Real,' he said. 'That was a great many years ago; but once you are Real, you can't become unreal again. It lasts for always.'

The Rabbit sighed. He thought it would be a long time before this magic called Real happened to him. He longed to become Real, to know what it felt like; and yet the idea of growing shabby and losing his eyes and whiskers was rather sad. He wished that he could become it without these uncomfortable things happening to him... [1]

Much like the Velveteen Rabbit and the Skin Horse, I am slowly becoming real. As God loves me through the crucible of my day, He offers many opportunities to become real, to become like Him in many wonderful ways. But sadly I do not take every opportunity that He offers. I do not love as He loves. I am much more selfish than selfless.

For example, my thoughtful enquiries via email may communicate to a friend something of God's selfless love. I do spend time thinking about my friend, and I genuinely want to know how they are getting on. This is real. This is like God. But my subtle and persistent refusal to engage socially with my friend probably shouts a different message. I prefer to relate on my terms, through my computer, keeping my friend at a distance and keeping me safe. Although dressed up as 'just the way I am made – a bit anti-social', the truth is that this is where my selfishness creeps in. This is where I refuse to become like my selflessly loving God. This is not real.

Could it be that some of the time I have modelled myself on someone or something else? This is the real problem. In subtle ways, I have refused the selfless love of God displayed in the death of His Son, and have simply found my own, less painful road in order to become.

This is my predicament: that because I am actually made to be in His image and not someone else's, only God's less travelled, selfless road will do. The truth is that as a human being, becoming like Christ in His death is the only way I become truly myself. Every other, more travelled, more comfortable, man-made road leads to unreality and therefore a deeply felt emptiness, frustration and disappointment.

This predicament is not just mine, but also ours together as a community. Church is designed to model herself on the family of the Trinity, and so become the warmly responsive bride of Christ, and the physical temple in which His Spirit dwells. Some of this is true, some of this is happening. But the fact is that the Church and her denominational systems have at the same time tended to become something else as well: multi-media corporations, controlling dictatorships, preservers of architecture or social clubs.

As Christian individuals and as a community of faith, none of us can deny that the messages we give are very mixed.

The message

'This is the message we have heard from Him and declare to you: God is light; in Him there is no darkness at all' (1 Jn 1:5).

God, unlike me, is light without darkness. He is just one thing: Himself. There is no mixed message. There is not a scrap of darkness or deception or shame or difficulty in self-expression in God. He is completely and purely genuine.

Everything exposed to light suddenly becomes visible. Glorious colour is revealed whilst shadows and darkness are discovered in contrast. In the same way, when our holy and uncreated God reveals Himself in full through His Son Jesus Christ, He also reveals everything else: the good, the bad, and the indifferent. His genuineness is the plumb line by which all other reality or façade is measured. What about you and I?

'If we claim to have fellowship with him yet walk in the darkness, we lie and do not live by the truth. But if we walk in the light, as he is in the light, we have fellowship with one another, and the blood of Jesus, his Son, purifies us from all sin' (1 Jn 1:6–7).

Fellowship means an active, mutual participation in relationship. It is not just a vague connection through association, but a genuine openness, a sharing heart to heart, an honest and real communication without games or defences. Fellowship is unity, a oneness of heart. Here in his first letter, the apostle John is directly challenging my hypocrisy when I say one thing and then do another. Like the Pharisees before me, I am two-faced, hiding my sin behind the mask of my public face, giving an outward appearance of holiness.

As I try to speak out the gospel, do I 'walk my talk' in my relationship with God? The truth is that mostly I foolishly believe that I can hide myself from Him. Deep down I am desperately ashamed. If I really walked in the light with God, being genuine about what goes on inside me and about the attitudes of my heart, then I would have to face the truth that He already sees me as I am: gloriously made in His image but utterly ruined by my own sin. I would have come face to face with my inner mess and then consciously choose either dependent helpless trust or independent self-reliance. But rather than take this painful journey, mostly I prefer to solve my problems my own way.

I pretend. Hiding behind what I foolishly believe is a more acceptable mask, I aim to convince everyone that there is actually nothing wrong. I respond to both God's and your enquiry of *'How are you?'* with *'I'm fine, thanks'* where 'fine' actually stands for fed up, indifferent, neurotic and exhausted. What I am really thinking is something like: *'Go away, I can't be bothered to tell you because actually you don't really want to know, and anyway I don't really want* to have to face how bad things are for me. I am profoundly disappointed with myself and with you. If you had any idea how little I care about anything that really matters to you, you'd be so shocked that you'd never want to talk to me again. I'm not OK and you're not OK and I can't bear that.'

The consequence is that I fail to receive and enjoy the legitimate intimacy that God intends for me, both with Him and you. Real intimacy in a graciously beloved fallen world is based on the premise that it is actually OK right now for both you and me to be faulty, simply because Jesus is not. The more I trust in this solution, the more I can be honest with God, walking in the light as He is in the light: at the cross. As I receive His mercy and healing there, the more I can become honest and open with you, because in Christ I am OK and so are you, and God is sorting the problem. It is as simple and as profound as that.

Real honest intimacy with God is the very source of our life and real honest intimacy among His people is how God proclaims His good news to a fallen world. We are His *message*, and mostly we have missed our true purpose for creation:

> *...and this is real and eternal life: that they know You, the one and only true God, and Jesus Christ, whom You sent... I spelled out Your character in detail to the men and women You gave Me... The message You gave Me, I gave them; and they took it, and were convinced that I came from You...the goal is for all of them to become one heart and mind just as You, Father, are in Me and I in You, so that they may be one heart and mind with Us. Then the world might believe that You, in fact, sent Me. The same glory You gave Me, I gave them, so they'll be as unified and together as we are, I in them and You in Me. Then they'll mature in this oneness, and give this godless world evidence that you've sent Me and loved them in the same way You've loved me.*
>
> John 17, *The Message*

In other words, Christian fellowship, the promised by-product of absolute honesty with God, is the way God chooses to proclaim the gospel. We are the *message*. So why does my non-Christian neighbour, for whom I have prayed long and hard, still stubbornly refuse to respond to our 'chats' about the gospel? Could it be that, although she hears my words about how good God is, she 'hears' a different message as she observes my behaviour in relationship with my Christian family and friends? My selfish actions give the game away. My tendency towards isolation and controlling behaviour all shout loudly that actually I am not at all sure that God is good and trustworthy. As she watches me steadfastly but unconsciously protect myself from harm, she might well conclude that God either is not what He is cracked up to be by the Christian community or does not even exist.

According to Jesus' prayer in John 17, the gift that God the Father has given me through Jesus Christ is eternal life: knowing Him, and being known by Him. In receiving that life through honest fellowship with Him, you and I then have a job to do. Our purpose as Church is to love each other so well that the world sees concrete evidence of the truth of God's goodness and love. When damage, danger and death seem to have the upper hand, folk often want the writing on the wall about God – hard facts which logically prove His existence and His goodness towards us. By the outworking of our relationship together in a community of faith, we are the evidence. Our role is to be full of grace and truth, accepting one another despite our sin, simply because of Jesus. This is our job this side of heaven; this is the core of evangelism. Our actions and behaviour in relationship with one another as Church speak far louder than any rousing speech or testimony we may offer to an unsaved world. The discipleship journey is as much about God forming a people who will be a light in darkness, ushering in His kingdom rule to an unsaved planet, as it is about freedom to become ourselves and so enjoy worshipping the living God. *Get Real!* is about evangelism from first to last.

So, just as St Francis of Assisi has said, you and I need to *'preach the gospel at all times – if necessary, use words.'* Interestingly enough, only 7% of the message I offer is through the actual words I use. The other 93% is transmitted through my voice tone and behaviour. In particular, when my body posture, facial expressions and behaviour are at odds with my spoken word, it is these that are 'read' and absorbed rather than my words. This means that roughly 93% of what I communicate about the gospel comes through my largely unconscious behaviour in relationships rather than what I say. Putting it bluntly, the way I say something is thirteen times 'louder' than the actual words I use. That is quite a shocking statistic.

If you can actually see my confusion and unbelief that clearly without me opening my mouth, then I may as well start talking about it. I may as well get real with God and with you. After all, neither of you are likely to be much surprised by what I say. As I respond to the penetrating light of God, I can begin to reject any lies I have foolishly believed and start to live out of God's version of reality: truth as He defines it. In this, I will discover something of who I actually am, my real self, the person I was designed to be before the creation of the world. As I get real about the ways in which I have avoided God's solution to the fall, I will begin to see clearly the less painful road I have chosen in order to become. This is about the development of my 'old' or false self, which once recognised can then be removed: *'Do not lie to each other, since you have taken off your old self with its practices and have put on the new self, which is being renewed in knowledge in the image of its Creator'* (Col 3:9–10).

Of course, I can choose to stay where I am in Christ with no condemnation, and continue in a relatively pain-free existence but with God and others only dimly on the horizon of my world. With few real selfless works to show for it, in such a position my faith is as good as dead. Alternatively, I can move out of the darkness into the light, take a risk and get real. The pain will probably get worse before it gets better, but I will also get the cleansing blood of Christ, a growing ability to be more genuinely myself and a tangible sense that both God and people are beginning to enter my world.

When I think about this, it is tempting to turn to you first and tell you all about your mask that is actually glaringly obvious to all of us that know you. But if I am unaware of my own mask, and have not first struggled to remove it, how can I help you with yours? No, the person I need to work on first is myself. It is painful to become more self-aware, and I do not like pain. I want to keep myself feeling comfortable. But actually, if I am going to become like Jesus, I need to examine who I am and how I relate from God's point of view, and face the pain of the process of change.

Probably much like you, I have foolishly convinced myself that the mask is the real me. I tend to see my apparent unsociable personality as who I am rather than a persona or false self used to protect myself from further disappointment or pain in relationships. Deep within I find myself questioning the wisdom of a god who apparently creates me unsociable and then leaves me with the consequent loneliness of living this way. Even deeper still, I see that I doubt the goodness or existence of a god who allows bad things to happen to apparently good people, and in particular to me. Right at the core, my faith in the holiness and goodness of a sovereign God is pretty much dead.

From that premise it is logical to hide the real me behind the covering of being anti-social. The real me longs to know and be known, I like to have fun with others, but mostly I long to be safe. I remain hidden to stop being hurt, but end up lonely and full of hatred of a so-called sovereign God who allows that hurt. Rather than enjoy fellowship with Him (and therefore with you), I tend to settle for the comfort and 'love' of hard work and its first fruit: achievement.

In reality, I barely know what I could be, satisfying myself with getting by with feeble attempts at acknowledging God and staying at a comfortable distance from both Him and you. Thankfully, He is far from satisfied, loving me too completely to leave me in that state. Day by day He encourages me to submit to the searching and cleansing of His Spirit. This loving Counsellor gently leads me into all the truth – the truth about God, the truth about others and the truth about myself. He longs that I respond to His gracious invitation to make me vibrantly real and therefore selfless like Jesus Christ.

I know that every day I must fight against my selfish ways of relating and respond to Him as He seeks to remove the armour plating of my mask. I need to learn to pray like David: *'Search me O God and know my heart. Test me and know my anxious thoughts. See if there is any offensive way in me, and lead me in the way everlasting'* (Ps 139:23–24).

More often than not, I am dim witted, blind and deaf to Him or else retort to His prompting with *'Clear off God, I'll live my life my own way'*. I realise now that I not only need the Holy Spirit, I need you. Just as the apostle Paul encouraged Timothy, I need you to remind me to watch my life closely, and I need you to watch it with me. I can only remove the part of the mask of which I am aware. I need you to make me aware. That is part of your task with me, as it is with me in relation to you. Be light to me, show up my darkness, be my mirror. As I risk telling you who I am (my thoughts, my opinions, my 'gut-level' feelings), I need you to listen. I also need your probing questions and your honest, compassionate observations. I need you to challenge, even confront me with who I try to appear to be. I also need to encounter you through your own vulnerability with me in order to somehow encounter myself. Be real with me. Share yourself. Let us enter each other's world.

This is what I hope *Get Real!* will provide – an opportunity to develop a deeper awareness of who you and I are as individuals and in our relationship with each other. As God opens our eyes to the masks of our pretence, we can then take a journey of discovery behind the facades and learn to see and accept ourselves as we really are: as Francis Schaeffer has said – both glorious and ruined. This process will take honest communication with ourselves, with each other and, above all, with God. We need this. To fulfil the great commission and see the coming kingdom of God, both you and I need the real me to be revealed. Both you and I need the same of you.

CHAPTER 2
WHAT IS REAL?

Superman. Is he a bird? Is he a plane? Is he a man? What about Clark Kent? Could he be the shy and retiring alter ego of our superhero, a mild-mannered newspaper reporter who literally works for both 'The Planet' and the planet? Which aspect of Clark is his true self: the defensive wimp or the multi-muscled saviour in tights? As the tale unfolds, Clark begins to discover his real nature as he receives the truth of where he came from and to whom he really belongs. Discovering his alien origins, his personal identity settles as he acknowledges and owns both his otherworldly parents and his otherworldly home. Being human is a lot like being the stammering Clark Kent with Superman bursting to get out. Like Clark, in order that I know who I am and what I am made for, I need to discover my true origins, the real source of my existence. To do that I first need to know how to determine whether or not my answers are correct. Is there an absolute? Who defines truth? Surely truth is relative?

The source and sustainer of all reality

Two thousand years ago Pontius Pilate posed the rhetorical question, *'What is truth?'* Like a tiny, unexpected raindrop falling into the great ocean of humanity's long search for meaning, Pilate's question formed ripples, echoes of the same question, throughout history, both backwards to Eden and forwards to the present day. Pilate's question stands at the centre, the crucial moment on which history hangs. Unknowingly, the Roman procurator practised his amateur philosophy before a man who, alone, is the living embodiment of the answer. Truth is a person: Jesus Christ.

Like Pilate, I can be a bit of an amateur philosopher and not actually expect such a thoroughly practical answer to my rhetorical question. Again, probably much like Pilate, I actually do not want answers. Mostly I just want to look good. After all, a tangible, personal response to the ultimate question 'What is truth?' would shock me into seeing that I actually need to do something. All the while, just as He did with Pilate, Jesus Christ simply waits before me, with no need of words, patiently, directly offering Himself in person as the answer to the ultimate question: *'I am the way and the truth and the life. No-one comes to the Father except through me'* (Jn 14:6).

If there is a personal Almighty who has created all things then logically He must be the living embodiment of truth and the one alone who defines what is true. To be almighty God He must be consistent, being what He says and does. More than this, He must be the only true God. It makes no sense for an ultimate power to be made up of many conflicting concepts or views. Such a disordered entity cannot be God as you and I define the word God. So, for those of us who believe in a supreme creative being, we know that He must be the ultimately reliable source of truth, a unique plumb line compared to which all else is out of true. Because He alone is God, His view is right. Other, differing views are wrong. That means that when I disagree with the Almighty, only one of us is right, and it's not me.

So, if almighty God exists, then He is truth. What does that truth look like? My first stab at an answer comes through looking at His signature in creation. From sub-atomic particle to the farthest star, dust has been moulded into wonderful, bizarre and even living shapes to get across His message in simple and vivid ways. In everything that I touch, see, smell, taste and hear, God is saying something about Himself.

I arrive at my second and more accurate understanding of God by looking at Scripture, His story within creation. Amazingly frank and intimate, I find that God is a person seeking to introduce Himself by name. A name is a powerful symbol for someone's personality, encapsulating and even sculpting identity. God's name in Hebrew is *Yahweh*, roughly explained as 'Yah the Living One' and expressed to Moses as 'I am who I am'. God is an 'I' rather than an 'it', with an identity or personality independent of any other source. Unlike me, He does not 'become' according to an external blueprint. He is. Quite simply, God's name tells me that He is the blue print, the source of existence and being, without need of anything or anyone outside Himself. Now that I find really hard to get my head around. God does not need me. Yet He invites me to relate to Him for the sheer pleasure of my company and for my own good. Sadly in deference to God's name, *Yahweh* is often translated as LORD and so much of its meaning is lost. Yet I need a constant reminder that God is *Yah the Living One*, the source of my life, so that I learn to fear His name through trust rather than avoidance.

Right through His creation story, there is an 'us-ness' to God in His self-description, a hint at community in His identity: *'Hear, O Israel: The LORD our God, the LORD is one'* (Deut 6:4).

The Hebrew word for 'one' here is *echod*, which means singularity with an internal structure. In other words, God is a compound unity. He is undivided and self-contained, without internal conflict, all of Him doing all that He does. Put another way, God really is a lot like light. Light from the sun seems simply to be 'white', but when this same sunlight enters and passes through raindrops in the air, I see a rainbow, the glorious wealth of different colours that have harmoniously blended together to make the whole 'white' light.

And so, as He continues with His story, God enters and passes through the raindrop of humanity in the person and work of Jesus Christ. God draws back the curtain on His 'oneness', revealing a Trinity of three persons: the Father, the Son and the Holy Spirit. Without contradicting Himself, God exists as a profound unity of three distinguishable, equal persons of the same substance. Each has His own role and context, His own place in this ultimate family unit. The Father is the ineffable head of the family. The only begotten Son is the Word or the *message* of God to creation, faithfully representing Him in every way. The Spirit proceeds from God into creation, bringing His life, forming and sustaining His order amid chaos, seeking to make His home within the physical realm. Father, Son and Holy Spirit function as a perfect, harmonious unity, structured by this internal order, bound together through loving relationship.

God is love, and the nature of His love is expressed between the members of the Trinity through selfless giving and warm receptivity with one another. God is oneness in community, the ultimate model for relationship between parent and child, and between a selfless partnership of equals: *'The Father loves the Son and gives him everything. The Son always does that which pleases the Father. The Spirit takes of the things of the Son and shows them to us. He does not glorify himself.'*[2]

So, real life (that is the self-existent life of God) is thoroughly relational. More than that, real life is 'oneness in community'. Oneness describes the nature of His family culture. Because God enjoys fellowship within Himself, we can conclude that it is not good (not of God) for Him to be alone. Although it may sound a little shocking because of the common use of the word, the Trinity is simply the way God expresses and fulfils His sexuality. When you and I talk of sexuality we usually think in physical terms. But fundamentally, sexuality is the longing to be not alone among equals. Since God is spirit, He expresses and fulfils this longing through the harmonious dancing movement of His oneness within His own community of equals.

Giving: the bold and glad selfless giving of the lover to the beloved, longing for impacting connection.

Receiving: the joyous and warm reception of the beloved to the lover, longing for fullness.

And, in the giving and the receiving, *completeness* comes (something more than if the lover or beloved were alone).

Who am I and what have I been made for?

Out of this wealth of other-centred relational love, there must be a creative outpouring. It is in the nature of love that it cannot be contained. It simply reproduces itself again and again. The love within the Trinity is an eternal fountain, passionately longing to bless, delight in and receive. But this same love also tumbles out of the Trinity, not as a trickle of leftovers after the family has had its fill, but as a cataract of other-centred blessing. God is Creator simply because He is love, selflessly and joyously creating community, reproducing something that looks a little like the Trinity, again and again: *'So God created man in his own image, in the image of God he created him; male and female he created them… God saw all that he had made, and it was very good'* (Gen 1:27, 31).

Quite simply, God has made bits and pieces of dust and filled them with His kind of life. Like a vast waterfall leaping down from a cliff far above the heavens, concentrating its descent upon a spot below, the life of God pounds down into humanity, made as a dependent vessel to receive, absorb and overflow with His blessing into all creation, faithfully representing Him through oneness in community: *'If anyone is thirsty, let him come to me and drink. Whoever believes in me… streams of living water will flow from within him'* (Jn 7:38).

If God *is* being then everything else only *has* being. As human beings, you and I are the pinnacle of God's loving creative endeavour. An image of His personhood is made physical in me; I am completely and helplessly dependent upon Him for every breath that I take. And so I am only because He is.

But mostly I see creation as having a life of its own, as if God had wound up the clock of the universe with sufficient internal energy to keep going independently without Him. I foolishly imagine that my next breath, my next heart beat, is up to me, not Him. In other words, He and I can go our own way and be unconcerned about one another. But that is not at all how God sees it.

The truth is that for my entire existence I remain a dependent creature. I have needs in relation to God that require fulfilment, like a child needing a parent. In God's order of things, in His version of what is real and true, He is my perfect parent providing for all my needs, and I am His child, receiving all that He offers. This is what it means for Him to be God. This is His role and function in relation to me as Creator to creature. This is also what it means to be a human being, my role and function in relation to him as creature to Creator. Recognising this difference in roles is what it means for me to put God in His rightful place.

As I step into and remain in my place of receptive rest and delight in His joyful provision, I am acknowledging, honouring and therefore worshipping who God is. In this place I love *Yahweh* with all my heart and soul and mind and strength. It follows that whatever or whoever I use to meet this spiritual 'parental' need is that which I have elevated to the position of my all-providing parent. By definition, this is my god.

Like Adam before me, I am designed to be neither self-existent nor self-sufficient. In this way I am not like God. I need. Everything about me depends upon Him and His grace towards me. Whether I like it or not, I am in His grip. And as I rest in that grip, I will receive what He gives: my existence and my unique personal identity (my real self). I am the subject of His desire, the very focus of His love, and because He is 'I am', I find that 'i am' too.

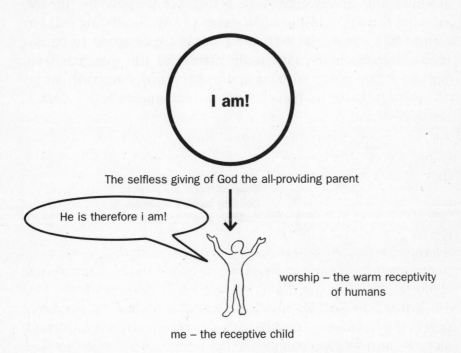

I am!

The selfless giving of God the all-providing parent

He is therefore i am!

worship – the warm receptivity
of humans

me – the receptive child

In his desire to tell His story in my life, God has filled my early days with dependency on physical parental figures. He wants to make sure I get the message about the nature of my relationship with Him. As a needy infant I sought dependency, motivated by a complex internal longing. Initially I longed to suckle at my mother's breast. As the nourishment and vitality of the milk filled me, I would have felt joy and contentment, basking in my mother's evident delight and loving attention. In its most faithful representation, this is a relationship of pure pleasure. God has designed me to experience a spiritual yet emotionally tangible version of that same pleasure in relationship with Him. Pleasure is what I am made for, that is why I crave it so much. True pleasure comes from complete dependency upon God. As I drink from God's fountain of living water in moment by moment dependency, a receptive creature resting in the loving gaze of an always giving Creator, I feel deep satisfaction and joy.

What is it exactly that God provides for me? What is this life, this spiritual parental love, this fullness that God seeks to pour into me? What is it that I thirst for?

Well, first I need a safe place to exist, then I need appropriate provision and finally I need an achievable purpose to aim for. These are the three fundamental needs of any developing child in relation to a parent. Further, these needs are designed to be fulfilled unconditionally. This is the nature of true parental love. Without a safe place, without appropriate provision, without an achievable purpose, human existence is fundamentally threatened.

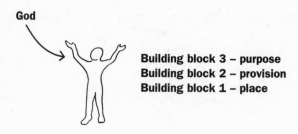

God

Building block 3 – purpose
Building block 2 – provision
Building block 1 – place

This is just how God loved Adam. Adam's foundational need was for security in his relationship with His Creator. In the Garden of Eden, Adam was given a place to be, where he belonged to God and was spiritually connected to Him. This was an environment of complete safety, where Adam could bask in the warmth of God's secure acceptance.

Having found his place to be, Adam was then offered the full and free provision for everything he actually needed (rather than what he wanted) both directly and through creation. In this he gained a sense of his value or worth to God as he saw the Lord lavishly providing for him in every way, even to the extent of giving guidelines or boundaries for his safe existence.

Finally, God educated Adam about his uniquely creative purpose as His steward within the Garden, working in it and taking care of it. Adam was given a job description and discovered that his role was to rule as God's representative, to bring His order to creation. In this way, God communicated to Adam that he was significant and irreplaceable in His economy. As God recognised and respected His unique workmanship in Adam, He allowed and encouraged Him to become an individual, his real self, bearing fruit with eternal impact. Adam's job was simple: to depend so profoundly upon God that he was then able to offer the world a taste of God's life, love and kingdom.

In the same way, in Paul's letter to the Ephesians, I am described as God's workmanship, created with a specific, predetermined purpose. The Greek word used here is *poiema* – the root word of our English word 'poem'. Could it be that I am a unique, irreplaceable poem from the heart of God? Could it be that you are too? Perhaps one reason that you and I are made differently is that we are designed to be complementary stanzas in God's eternal story, our diversity and difference weaving His own glorious counter-point. If this is the case then individual uniqueness is to be celebrated rather than seen as a source of conflict and division.

Maybe the unique poem He speaks out through you is saying something about His steadfast daily commitment. You might be the kind of person who is truly meant to represent God by your sheer sticking power. Maybe the unique poem He speaks through me shouts out something of His passionate belief in people. I might be the kind of person who has been particularly made to represent Him by believing in and encouraging even the most hopeless cases, spurring them on towards their destiny in Christ. Either way we are like Him, each telling just a part of His story so that together we reflect Him more fully.

I am His poem.
I am a gift from Him to you –
a personal message from the heart of God,
my very being speaking of His nature.
He is both author and emissary of this, His word to you.
Conceived in Mind, held in Heart,
spoken by the mouth of God –
I am in His grip.

I certainly have a job description, whether I work in the worldly sense or not. You and I each enjoy the unique role of bearing His image, literally glorifying or revealing Him by carrying His likeness individually and as community to all creation. It is an awesome thing to be human, God's masterpiece in creation, to be a carefully crafted, finite, communicable likeness of our infinite, incommunicable God.

Think of it. From the beginning of creation the planet has been populated with finite, dignified representations of the living God. Why does God command me not to build or create representations of Him? Surely it would be helpful to have something tangible to remind me of what He is like? But then I remind myself that God is so beyond human understanding that only He can adequately represent Himself. As I try to depict God through art or object, inevitably I get it wrong, I am too small to communicate God through my own small-minded creation. Only one thing can adequately do the job: you. Go and take a good look in a mirror right now or even at the person sitting next to you. What you glimpse may be the nearest thing to God you will see all day.

Who are we and what have we been made for?

That leads me to talk about the next part of my image-bearing as a human being. I am made for relationship with other people. As well as being created to receive individually from God, I am also designed to relate to other human beings, either as a dependent 'child', as a providing 'parent' or as an interdependent peer. Just as with individuals, different people groups (families, local communities, working teams, tribes and nations) are each designed to reflect just a small part of God's image. The diversity of human community shouts about the profundity of God's nature. Only the rich variety of people groups together can hope to reveal something of the Trinity.

At least two of my human relationships have been designed for me to be as a dependent child to a providing parent. I long to be appropriately parented by human beings who will represent God's parental love to me and to be set within a family structure and ethnic culture that reflects something wonderful about God. This parental responsibility is offered to my genetic parents, grandparents and wider family, teachers, local community, folk who have discipled me in church and in the work place, my nation and so on. My receptivity to the good bestowed upon me by human parental figures and the respect I offer them in return are all designed to communicate the honour and worship deserved by God as my spiritual parent. As a 'child', I am one of God's channels of communication.

Some of my human relationships are designed to be as a providing parent to others as my 'children'. Because I am like God, whether or not I have genetic children, I naturally find myself longing to parent others with an unconditional love in the context of family, work and ethnic structures: offering a safe place to exist, selflessly providing in appropriate ways and then helping my 'children' to become uniquely themselves. Suitable 'children' are my own genetic offspring, the kids in the Sunday school class I run, the folk I disciple and pastor, the more vulnerable members of the society in which I live. The way I nurture others is designed to communicate God's perfect and selfless love as their spiritual parent. As a 'parent', I am one of His channels of communication.

Finally, whatever age I am, many of my relationships will be with peers. These relationships with equals are designed to reflect the interdependent relationships of the Trinity: selflessly giving and warmly receiving. Like the members of the Trinity, it is not good for me to be alone among equals. I have a peer need for partnership, to be part of a team, to enjoy oneness in a diverse community of equals: friends of either gender, work mates with both similar and different ways of approaching problems, friends of similar and diverse ethnic and cultural origins, and maybe a life-long partner. The way I fulfil this longing for oneness is designed to communicate trinitarian love. As a 'peer', I am one of God's channels of communication. But this peer need is not so crucial to me as my parental needs. Without fulfilled parental needs, like many abandoned children, emotionally or even physically I will simply die.

In all this I am meant to be holy as God is holy. Like the persons in the Trinity, people are individuals with boundaries. This means that I am responsible for myself, my body, my feelings, my choices, my thoughts and my longings. There is a definite place (physically and in terms of responsibility) where I end and you start. My skin is even a helpful symbol of my individuality. I am

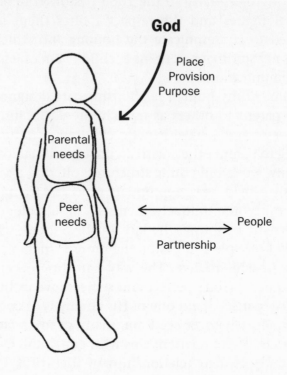

separate and therefore 'other' than you. Holiness means that we are to respect and honour each other's separateness, so that if you trespass against my boundary, you owe me a debt and vice versa.

Returning to God's story of His relationship with Adam, it was not good for Adam to be alone. He needed help. Carefully God drew out of Adam the realisation that there was no suitable helper for him among created beasts. In this way God pointed out human sexuality, made in the image of God's sexuality. This is the human yearning for oneness, to be united together in a community of equal human beings. God's intention is that human community looks like the Trinity. With an equality of nature, together we are designed to form a harmonious unity, structured by an internal order, with different roles and joyfully bound together through a remarkable other-centred love, a sharing of selfless giving and warm receptivity, rather than gratification of individual need.

Perfect all-providing parent – the source and sustainer

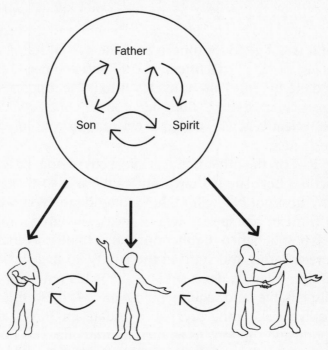

Each person *receives* from God.
Each person *relates* to others through selflessly giving and warmly receiving.
Each person *rules* appropriately over creation.

According to God, male and female together as embodied beings reflect Him best. This could be a rather startling revelation to some of us. How can God be like a woman, surely He's a bloke? After all, He calls Himself Father, and Jesus came as a man not a woman, and even the Holy Spirit is referred to as 'He'. But as we peel away the layers of cultural interpretation of Scripture, I think God is trying to help us see that although He is fundamentally the selflessly giving Father, the courageously masculine Son, and the guiding and directive Holy Spirit, He does have feminine as well as masculine qualities. Particularly in His parental attitude towards us, He has both a mother's and a father's heart.

Men and women are designed to experience an equality of

nature, an inbuilt defined order, and an inbuilt difference of role and context. Adam is made out of dust. The planet is his context, his particular area of focus, the environment in which he is best designed to function. His role there is to selflessly love, ruling and reigning as God's steward, as he tends, orders and subdues creation. But God has told him (and therefore all the rest of you guys) that it is not good for him to be alone in that ruling and reigning. It is just not godly. Gentlemen, God says you need help! The job is not done the way God wants it without the support of others, and in particular women, alongside you as your equals. Learning to relate effectively with others is essential to your job of bringing in God's order.

Eve, on the other hand, is made out of Adam. Genesis 2:22–23 describes how she is drawn out of his side so that she is neither above him nor below him, but alongside in every way. People are her context, her special area of focus, the environment in which she is best designed to function. Just as there is a difference in roles between Father and Spirit in the Trinity, so there is between Adam and Eve. Adam is her head and she is his responsive, supportive, indispensable and equal 'help-mate'. Ladies, this means that broadly speaking the guys get to initiate and direct, and you get to respond and support. As women we find ourselves functioning out of context unless somewhere along the line there is a man 'covering' us and inviting us to help him in some way. We are not designed to initiate alone. The revelation and rule of God in creation fundamentally comes through men and women relating in team together, focusing on the planet and the people according to our inbuilt but different purpose and gifting.

In God's economy for humanity, gender is at the very core of my personal identity and affects the way in which I am designed to relate to others and to my environment. Taking a look at how we literally physically fit together as men and women, we might take this as a symbol for the deeper reality of what it actually means to be a male or female.

Just as Adam seems designed to reflect the selfless, bold love of God, so Eve is designed to display His warmly supportive and receptive beauty. Together, as king and queen of creation, the image of God is complete and the effect is breathtaking. Whether I am male or female, my gender identity is formed from a composite balance of my masculine and feminine qualities. Put very

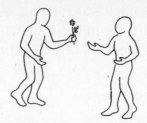

The essence of **maleness** is:	The essence of **femaleness** is:
• The ability to selflessly give.	• The capacity to warmly receive.
• To initiate and bless.	• To nurture and contain.
• Bringing order out of chaos.	• Creatively bringing forth into being.

simplistically, the more I tend to initiate and order, the more masculine I seem. The more I tend to creatively nurture, the more feminine I seem. Usually the balance of these will vary from one context to another.

Within human community, God has made our life like His by giving us gender. Because we are physical, that not only makes possible general human sexuality but also genital human sexuality. In other words, male and female have been separated by God in order to enjoy and communicate 'oneness in community' and, in certain contexts, 'one flesh'. Scripture indicates that God has given sex as a specific tool to fulfil the longing for oneness among equals in the very specific context of a marriage covenant, where the barrier of difference and separateness is allowed to be broken completely.

Sex is not intended to keep me secure, nor to give me a sense of worth, nor even purpose. These are all parental needs with their own specific tools to fulfil them (like a home or an education or a role in a local community). No, in the context of marriage, sex is intended to wonderfully cross the barrier of separateness, offering a living picture of Christ's passionate desire for interdependent union with His bride, the Church. As the apostle Paul says, given who God is and who we are, this is a mystery! But what we can say is that sex seems designed to be about a union of opposites, selflessly blessing and warmly receiving, giving not getting, receiving not refusing.

Surely this must be our other spiritual thirst of which human, interdependent relationship is only a reflection: the spiritual peer need to unite with Christ as the beloved to her lover. For it is only as we truly are the dependent children of Father God choosing to obey Him and honour Him as He is that we can mature to become the beloved of His only begotten Son, Jesus Christ. Finally, in the consummation of all things, in God both needs will be completely fulfilled.

CHAPTER 3
THE FALL FROM REALITY

Even the most cursory glance at my own inner workings and my somewhat feeble attempts at relationship leave me in no doubt that something has gone seriously wrong with my image-bearing as an individual. When I look at groups of people, I am forced to come to the same conclusion about human community in general. Individually and corporately, none of us look much like God. Something has gone desperately wrong. But what?

The covenant

Turning again to God's unfolding story in the world, I see that from the beginning, God has sought to educate people about our relationship with Him through the use of something called covenant. A covenant is a binding agreement offering a promise of blessing under certain conditions and expectations, repeatedly used to define the nature of the personal relationship between God and His dependent creation. This covenant or promise is basically summarised as: *'You will be My people, and I will be your God.'* In other words, as we depend on Him as the sole provider of our needs, we will represent Him effectively to creation. We will be *His* people.

Once Adam was brought into a natural, creaturely relationship with God, he needed educating about the pre-determined nature of his human existence. Then, with open eyes, he might fully and freely enter into his special inheritance. David Atkinson puts it well: *'the immature dependency of his life on the gift of God's breath is intended to grow into the mature dependency of obedience to God's life-giving Word.'*[3]

And so the discipleship of Adam began: *'The Lord God took the man and put him in the Garden of Eden to work it and take care of it. And the Lord God commanded the man, "You are free to eat from any tree in the garden; but you must not eat from the tree of the knowledge of good and evil, for when you eat of it you will surely die"'* (Gen 2:15–17).

With Adam as our head and us as his 'seed', humankind was

offered a stable home, abundant provision, and a job description. This was not just for a season either, but eternally. In planting the tree of the knowledge of good and evil so that Adam and Eve could eat the fruit, God clarified His condition for this gift of eternal life: our helpless dependence upon Him. This was the 'skin' that separated humanity from God: a breakable, tangible boundary describing the difference while inviting co-operation through mutual trust and respect of our particular degrees of holiness and sovereignty. Through Adam, God has warned us that the knowledge of both good and evil would render us insecure and disconnect us from Him. However, not eating that particular fruit would demonstrate trusting, dependent obedience and so our place in Him would be secure for ever.

And so we discovered that we had freedom of choice: to obey or to disobey, to be or not to be according to God's rules. Having made us in His image, God would not disrespect or deny that image within us. He would not imprison us within an environment of absolute safety (the fruit safely out of reach). In that position we could neither hurt God nor ourselves, nor relate sovereign to Sovereign but only like a puppy dog to a master. He simply respected us too much. Nor would He tolerate relationship with us whatever our behaviour ('pick the fruit if you like'). He respected Himself too much. Instead, He bravely and selflessly sought the vulnerability of intimate relationship with a creature capable of choice both for Him and against Him.

With the tree of the knowledge of good and evil in sight, Adam had a spectator's knowledge of what is good (of God, perfect) and what is evil (spoilt, broken in pieces). To respect the boundary was good. To disrespect it was evil. What he did not have was the taste of the fruit in his mouth, the nutrients in his belly. God said this intimate knowing (union with) both good and evil would kill Adam. In other words he would lose his place (and provision and purpose), be put outside the Garden and be subject to the natural order like any other animal.

As dependent children, humans were designed to taste only goodness (what is of God, perfection). Eating the fruit of the tree acted like a visible skin between dependent creation and the independent Godhead, giving us a loud and clear message: *Because I am other than you, because I am Creator, it is Mine to intimately 'know' the knowledge of both good and evil, not yours. You cannot 'know' this knowledge and yet live, so don't even try. Trust Me in this. Bearing alone this 'knowing' is the way that I show you that I am set apart from you. It is a sign of My holiness that I 'know' the knowledge of both good and evil yet I am and will remain thoroughly good.*

The fall from reality

Together at last, Adam and Eve relaxed in the heat of the day. God was apparently not in the Garden; He was unseen. Like a mother playing hide-and-seek with a baby by momentarily covering her face with her hands, God was encouraging them to hold on to the constancy of His love even when they could not see Him face to face. His behaviour invited dependence on His word, rather than His face-to-face presence.

Adam and Eve were then tested in their response to God's boundary. Satan, the accuser, turned up and started a conversation with Eve, who was in a weaker position having only received the condition of the covenant second-hand through Adam. Like an old gossip, Satan wildly exaggerated the boundary to draw out her comparatively minor doubt about God's desire to provide: *'Did God really say "You must not eat from any tree in the Garden"?'* Baited by the enemy, Eve corrected the accusation but offered a slightly enlarged boundary: from not eating the fruit to not touching the tree either. Eve seems to have invented religion. Like her descendents the Pharisees, and out of doubt in God, she had already mentally added to the rules in an attempt to manage her provision in her own way, through control.

The trap was set: *'You will not surely die. For God knows that when you eat of it your eyes will be opened, and you will be like God, knowing good and evil.'* Listening to Satan, Adam and Eve were tempted to doubt the genuineness of God and instead believe firstly that this 'god' was a liar and was withholding something beneficial from them. In other words, this 'god' was not good. Secondly like this 'god' they could be independent and enjoy the knowledge of both good and evil. So this 'god' was not holy. Adam and Eve could infer that the boundary was there to make this 'god' seem special in their eyes when in fact he was not. In other words this 'god' wore a mask and had such an inferiority complex that he had to try to seem superior to others.

Remembering their image-bearing, I can imagine that if Eve believed this she then looked at Adam and saw the same inferiority, the same sham. Maybe she looked at herself and saw worthlessness because this 'god' was simply unable to provide the best. In other words, she seems to have wrongly believed that this 'god' was not OK, so they were not OK and were therefore in need. Without any reference to her partner, she looked at the fruit and saw it as good for her not toxic, as a source of pleasure not pain, as increasing her wisdom not dulling her thinking. And so she chose to eat to fulfil her own parental needs and also provide for Adam in the same way, who was with her all along. One half of the partnership, created to function in the context of the other as a responsive, receptive helpmate, initiated alone as a 'controller' to parentally provide for both herself and her husband. Her actions made a declaration of self-dependence: *I will get life my own way.*

The other half of the partnership, called to selflessly initiate in the life of his companion, remained passively receiving that provision she had claimed. Called to represent God to Eve, why would Adam choose to sit back and do nothing? His inaction arose from the same mistaken perception of God: if this 'god' is inferior, he is useless as a source of significance, which rendered Adam inferior and needy too. If he played the 'compliant child' to Eve's 'controlling parent', he would avoid further failure in her eyes and so at least maintain his current rather low level of self-respect. His chosen passivity made a similar declaration of self-dependence: *I will protect my life my own way.*

The 'skin' or boundary between Creator and creation was then penetrated in full as the head of the human race ate the fruit seeking to be 'like God'. Gender identity had been turned on its head. Dependent and interdependent relationships were ruined. The covenant was broken. The pot had denied dependency on the potter and declared *I will make myself.*

Like a foetus cutting its own umbilical cord, or a small child crawling out of the family home and expecting to survive, humankind and its kingdom fell from the grip of God as Adam's choices were respected. The fall came about by the denial of helpless dependence upon a holy God, and by a declaration of self-dependence. This is our most basic and original sin. As Adam's descendants, it still infects us all.

Why choose independence? Well, independence feels better

because I gain autonomy, finding my own way to meet my needs. Doubting God, I dare not trust in His provision, and will often do anything to avoid the confusion and helplessness of dependency upon someone I see as not having my best interests at heart or even impotent to come through for me. Forsaking God as He is and His word to me, I choose another definition of reality (who God is and who I can be). The pride and demand of my new 'father' is seeded in me. No longer drawing my life from 'I am who I am' (God), I take it from the enemy. Satan has chosen independent autonomy as his life source: 'i will therefore i am' and so, as his 'child', I respond with 'i will too'.

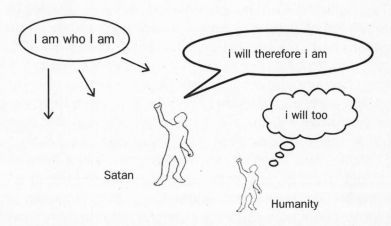

I caught a glimpse of the fall, as if through the eyes of Adam and Eve, the night after my father died. Only a few weeks previously, my father had come to live with us. Now I lay wakeful on a duvet next to my husband, surrounded by our children in small, sleepy heaps upon the floor. With the shock of this sudden family death, we spontaneously sheltered the night together. We knew our frailty and our need of one another. In some deep recess of our souls, we found ourselves frightened by that which no human fully expects or is completely prepared for. Like Adam and Eve before us, at a deep level we had not really believed that death would come to us.

As I mouthed silent words to God, I experienced His kingdom draw so close to me that I felt I could reach out and touch the absolute, defining beauty of heaven. Beauty that could be felt rather than seen was novel to me. I was caught up with what seemed like an endless moment.

I woke with a start some hours later to my first morning in a world without my human father. The beauty of the night before had gone. I felt like I had fallen away from heaven. It dawned upon me that the pain of separation from my father was nothing, absolutely nothing, compared with my experience of having 'fallen' overnight from the tangible beauty of the presence of God. I began to recognise how far, how very far, humankind and creation fell from intimacy with God that day long ago in the Garden of Eden. My senses were intensely focused. Looking out of the window, the world seemed deadened beyond belief, bearing only a very faint thumbprint of its Creator.

For the first time I saw how my spirit, which was then straining to recapture the real presence of God, was daily drugged by my addiction to independence. Like all creation around me, from the very moment of my conception I had fallen an infinite distance, separated from the source of my life by a gigantic vertical chasm that no effort of mine could surmount.

About a week later, I found myself slowly returning to my previous insensitivity to the fall, both within me and around me. I looked at the world and thought we had made it a pleasant and comfortable place when in fact, under our so-called stewardship, the planet has actually become one huge, dried-up, bombed-out, concrete bunker. I saw myself rationalising that my hidden strategies for sustaining my existence were sensible and even good tactics in relationship. Independence felt right. Once again I was separating myself from the intoxicating beauty of God by my own choices for a quick fix of whatever was immediately at hand and believable as a source of life. I had all too easily become satisfied with dross and had completely forgotten what real sustenance and beauty looked and felt like.

Thankfully the fall and the incalculable losses it has incurred generation by generation are not where the story ends. For as God walked in the Garden in the cool of the day, once again He pursued face-to-face communion with His people: *'Where are you?'* From behind both a covering of fig leaves and a tree as an extra insurance policy, Adam responded with: *'I was afraid because I was naked so I hid.'* Before the fall, being genuinely and freely ourselves in our physically naked state was not a source of shame. We saw the real God as He is, without façade and we believed He was OK. Being made in His image, we could be like Him, uncovered, genuinely ourselves and OK. But then humankind's eyes were opened to evil as well as good. Suddenly we believed this creator 'god' to be 'naked' in the second sense: needy, impoverished and rather helpless behind his own 'mask' of the imposed boundary. If he was 'naked' in this way, then so were his image-bearers. We were not OK. In the presence of each other both then in the Garden of Eden and now, our perceived inferiority triggers intense personal shame. Physically and relationally, we still craft a covering of 'fig leaves' – the masks we wear to hide the emptiness and to persuade others to accept, provide for and respect us.

In the presence of this 'god' that we see with our eyes opened to evil, we feel fear. We expect law and punishment without grace and love. To protect ourselves from the inevitable disconnection, we hide away behind creation, avoiding face-to-face conversation with this 'god', usually preferring to ignore him altogether. Like a hidden, life-long, terminal disease, independence ruins every attitude of my heart. At the core, I am selfish, deceitful, and thoroughly empty, thirsting for a place, provision and purpose in someone or something that I can subtly control.

Surely, you say to yourself, the death and resurrection of Jesus Christ redeems me back into full relationship with God? Well, because Jesus Christ has satisfied the condition of God's covenant with Adam, God has graciously declared that Christ's obedience is all that is necessary for me to unconditionally receive the blessing of that covenant. Therefore, from the eternal perspective and through an active faith in Jesus Christ, my 'nakedness' is covered by Christ, I am justified before God and I can be filled with the living water of His Holy Spirit. I can once again receive eternal life: a place, provision and a purpose for ever.

But I am not yet fully Christ-like. In his letter to the Romans, Paul reminds me that some of the time my mind is subtly hostile to God and some of the time I am more in step with the desires of the Spirit. So the fruit I develop and offer to others is a very mixed bag. Like the Pharisees, I am mostly blind to the deceit in my heart and have almost no idea how far I have fallen. I still work hard to get you to fill me up rather than turn to God. I want you to accept me, provide for me and respect me. Even my best intention in prayer is usually ruined by independence: *Dear God: please help my neighbour to know you better (they do need that, God, and besides which, then I'll be a successful Christian in the eyes of others and so peo-*

ple will think I'm OK). God will never answer this and similar prayers because of my attitude of heart. He is simply not interested in sustaining my independence.

Putting it another way, imagine a gorgeous glove of the finest leather fashioned in the image of a particular hand that is both beautiful and strong. Empty of its living content, the glove is elegant and interesting to inspect, hinting at the beauty and strength of the hand. Alone, it has no real being or substantial significance. Once filled by the hand, it becomes connected to the point and source of its existence and acts as directed from within with dignity, power and purpose. It now functions fully in transmitting the message of the hand. Beauty and strength are proclaimed.

As a human being, I am a lot like that glove. Incredibly, I bear the honour of being made in the likeness of the living God. Divorced from Him through my own independence, like the glove I am emptied and cannot function as designed. The consequence of my independence is that every aspect of me has been spoilt. I attempt to fill myself with anything that I believe is a controllable source of life. It might be achievement or attachment to people or food or sexual gratification or even being pleasant. The list of possibilities is endless. In reality I cannot satisfy my need with something other than God, because only God can fill a God-shaped hole. Inevitably I experience misery, confusion, pain, hopelessness and profound disappointment. *'My people have committed two sins: They have forsaken me, the spring of living water, and have dug their own cisterns, broken cisterns that cannot hold water'* (Jer 2:13).

When I first invited Jesus into my life, inevitably there was an incomplete repentance. It is as if I asked the hand to enter me as a glove, amid a lot of mess sloshing about inside. But even as the restoration process began, I found that old habits die hard. Unconsciously I have often continued to pursue those wrong sources of 'life': the acceptance of others, their admiration, the comfort of food or achievement and so on. Within me, I leave little room for God. So, when I relate to you, often what spills out is a mixture of the muddied water of my broken cistern together with the stream of living water that God intends. This is not the Christian life. This is a compromise.

Why won't I turn to God alone when all my visible, controllable sources of life are actually so ineffective at providing my needs? Jesus offers me the answer: *'I am the bread of life. He who* comes to me will never grow hungry, and he who believes in me will never be thirsty. But as I told you, you have seen me and still you do not believe' (Jn 6:35–36).

What's gone wrong with us?

So it is my thinking that is the core problem. But before I explore that in depth, it may be useful to see how other areas of my being have been impacted by the fall. Designed to reveal God and His nature, independence has actually affected every part of my image-bearing. In my body, my feelings, my choices, my thoughts and my deep spiritual longings, the *message* has become corrupted.

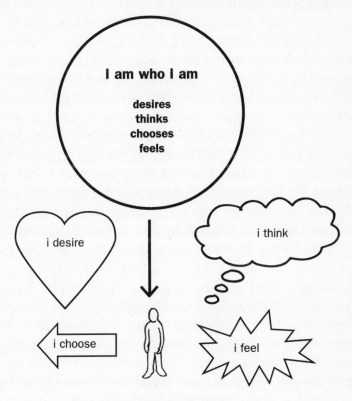

All in a created body

Because of the fall, I am physically disabled in some way, however minor, and my human body degenerates and eventually dies. As a result of this universal problem, Western culture spends a vast sum of money every year to keep further disability and death at bay. While it is entirely appropriate to fund medical and palliative care, and maintain a healthy lifestyle, some of us try to go much further and attempt to permanently fix the physical consequence of the fall. The extremes of twenty-first century medical research seem to express our insatiable demand to be independent and still enjoy eternal life, even when all the odds are physically stacked against us. The truth is that no one but God can give eternal life, and stupidly we still believe the serpent: surely we will not die! In reality my complex design cannot be maintained by human effort alone. Like the rest of the universe, having been set in order out of the chaos, the consequence of separation from my maker is that physically I wind down to disorder and base elements once again. Therefore, outside the gracious action of God, independence means I cannot evolve but only devolve, becoming less like God not more.

What about emotions? Like God, I enjoy a capacity to feel deeply when I encounter my world. As His image-bearer, my emotions are designed to be acknowledged and owned as my responsibility, welcomed as a fundamental part of being alive and fully and appropriately expressed, revealing the emotional heart of God.

Scripture widely refers to God's emotions: joy, delight, pleasure but also grief and raging anger. One of the most profound and certainly the shortest verse in Scripture reveals the empathetic heart of God become Man when face to face with death in His Creation, the ultimate result of the fall. As Jesus weeps outside the tomb of Lazarus, I glimpse at God's capacity to deeply feel my plight. Suddenly I am not alone in my sorrow at the grim consequences of the fall. God steps into my shoes, He sees the world through my eyes, feels my feelings and echoes back His profound understanding through the grief of His Son.

But what has independence done to the emotional content of the *message*? As I bump into my world, what I feel may be legitimate, but it is what I do with my feelings that gets me into trouble. Probably the first thing I do is disown them, blaming someone or something else: *'You made me feel.'* Nobody and nothing makes me feel anything. You are not responsible for my feelings, I am. My emotions are my unique, personal response to my internal and external world. They are to do with me, not you. My denial of this fact negates one of the most important and wonderful aspects of the *message*. I rob myself of who I am.

The second thing I tend to do with my emotions is to bury them. Life in a fallen world has taught me that full emotional expression does not bring the hoped-for response from others. I fall silent and lock up my unwanted or unanswered feelings in an emotional back room. Avoiding experiences that would trigger similar emotional reactions, I condition myself to pursue short-term comfort at all costs. Perhaps unrealistically I even long for a complete absence of uncomfortable emotions, burying the lot so that in some kind of living death I barely feel at all. Maybe then my buried emotions actually make me ill through their biochemical impact on the various body organs where emotional memory is now known to be stored.

But when life unexpectedly squeezes me like a toothpaste tube, I suddenly become aware that I am on the edge of feeling. Like a dormant but very much alive virus, every now and then I break out in a sudden fever of emotion. Usually I stuff my feelings back into my emotional back room, lock the door, throw away the key, and pretend that nothing has happened. Why do I do this? Probably I only dimly realise that my emotional over-reaction is neither relevant nor healthy as a response to my current experience.

What I tend to ignore is that my deeply buried emotions are understandable when felt at their point of actual origin, perhaps as a response to a forgotten childhood experience. Insecure attachment to others triggers concern, anxiety, fear, terror and even shock, depending upon the degree of insecurity. Reduced self-esteem through neglect can arouse irritation, anger, rage and even hatred. Finally, insignificance through apparent failure or inferiority triggers guilt, embarrassment and shame.

For me, one of the biggest and most troublesome occupants of my emotional back room was an infant scream of shock and terror, a buried reaction to a sudden insecurity in relationship with my mother when I was just a few weeks old. Like a giant constantly rumbling, banging and hollering at the door, I have felt the pangs of that particular terror all my life. Any sudden exposure to potential rejection and disapproval would wake up my giant. In the end, by the grace of God, I chose to face up to him, open the door, let him out into the light and fully express him in the right context of my life-story and into the body of Jesus on the cross.

Nowadays if a friend expresses healthy disappointment with

my part in our relationship, my emotional response is usually more like concern than terror, embarrassment than shame. I see them as not necessarily wanting to reject me and judge me but woo me towards positive change. Suddenly I become painfully aware of my reactions towards them and we are experiencing real communication. This is not comfortable for either of us but it is healthy. It is the *message*. Amazingly we are glorifying God, revealing Him in our relationship together.

One night, a number of years ago, God kept me awake to talk to me. He seemed to tell me something very simple yet profound: *'Ros, you hate people.'* Outside observers may well have been confused by this. I seemed to love both my family and God's people tolerably well and displayed a keen interest in social and environmental concerns. But I was not confused, I was convicted.

What was God talking about? I believe He was referring to my deep emotional reaction to others that I covertly expressed in my more subtle behaviour in relationships: withdrawal from vulnerable intimacy, occasional bursts of demanding anger and my flight into being alone. At a deep level I did not care. I had become a hater of others and a lover of myself as day by day I let the sun go down on my anger and grew indifferent to people. In the depth of my heart there was a complete absence of warm, godly compassion.

You see, God did not have a problem with my anger as such, but what I did with it. When faced, felt and rightly expressed, hot anger would have helped me recognise something was amiss. On the other hand, my indifference seemed so normal that I remained unmotivated to change. When I heard God talk about this, I believed Him. He was right, there was no point in hiding any more. Together He and I have begun to explore and express the roots of that indifference. By the grace of God, I will learn to love. And why was I angry in the first place?

Like everyone else, I have experienced disappointment in all my relationships. Nothing and no one seems to have given to me as they should. I am even disappointed with God because I imperfectly receive all that He has to offer. Worse still, for His own reasons, His redemption plan unfolds slowly, subjecting me to frustration that I rarely handle well. I want full salvation now!

God, on the other hand, longs for me to handle my anger as He does: acknowledging and carefully suppressing His righteous wrath, holding it to one side without burying it, until the moment comes when He rightly and fully expresses it in the body of His Son. His healthy emotional suppression and expression makes room for His love alongside His wrath, His joy alongside His grief, His pleasure alongside His disappointment.

What about choices? God is almighty. He is sovereign. He wills. He sets His goal. He acts to achieve that goal. As an image-bearer, I also have the capacity to choose; I am a little sovereign over my own kingdom for which I am given responsibility. What I do is therefore what I choose to do. But my freedom of choice is limited as almighty God keeps me within the boundaries He has set. He asks that I represent His rule and authority through my chosen behaviour. With full respect for His own image, He will not protect me from the known consequences of disobeying Him. Like God, I choose aims and objectives for my life and the necessary behaviour to ensure I achieve those aims, all under His sovereign plan. And what is my aim meant to be? Why, the same aim as His, of course: His glory, the enjoyment of the revelation of God from first to last.

So how has independence affected my capacity to choose and my awareness of my choices? Without realising it, my aims and behaviours in relationship are mostly self-centred rather than other-centred. In this life I tend to want comfort not Christ, happiness not holiness. Short-term gratification of my needs to manage emotional discomfort has taken precedence over delaying gratification to pursue eternal joy.

Whatever or whoever looks most likely to provide for my comfort and happiness in a way that is under my control, that is what I will ruthlessly milk. Like a baby that has aborted herself from the womb of God, I am seeking a self-made, controllable place of provision. When I find it, I plug in my spiritual umbilical cord and try to get what I need. What is it that looks most like God yet can be manipulated to my own ends? Ah... there you are! Yes, you! You people made in the image of God – you will do nicely as a source of life, or at least you will do well enough to ensure that I achieve what is most important to me, my autonomy. However useless you are at giving me what I desperately need, I would rather suffer near starvation at my core than submit to the indignity of helpless dependence. Even as a Christian, in some parts of my heart I refuse to admit I have made a mistake in choosing independence, and instead require that other people or things meet my parental needs for safe attachment, approval and significance. Without consciously realising it, these have become my life-goals.

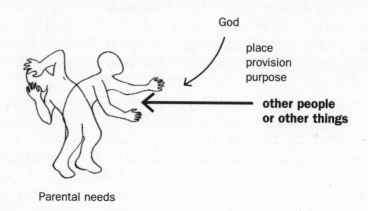

One of the consequences of my independence is that my life-goals are mostly unrecognised. I am blind to the depth of my self-centredness in relationship and have lost the conscious knowledge of what I am actually aiming for. Therefore I experience my actions and behaviour as mostly compulsive. Although what I do is what I choose to do, I have largely lost my awareness of that choice.

If I am hungry for safe connection, then I will tend to set this as a life-goal to manage my anxiety. What behaviour can I employ to get a guaranteed place in your life? Perhaps by refusing to challenge any of your unhelpful behaviour or by rescuing you when you are needy, I will keep you so pleased with me that the risk of you rejecting me is reduced to a minimum.

If I hunger for self-esteem, then I will tend to set this as a life-goal to manage my anger. What can I do to get you to provide so well for me that I am comfortably convinced of my worth in your eyes? Perhaps I play the needy victim to your ardent rescuer, enticing you to put yourself out for me. As I see you making repeated and costly efforts on my behalf, you confirm that I am worthwhile. Alternatively I may flee from relationship with you altogether. If I never allow you an opportunity to give to me, I will never have to suffer the disappointment of how poorly you supply my needs. In this way, although my self-esteem is low, I can maintain it at a level I am used to.

If I hunger for purpose, then I will tend to set this as a life-goal to manage my shame and guilt. I might choose to achieve near perfectly in my profession through ambitious over-activity. The triumphs of my achievements, your respect, compliments and deference to my evident superiority all give me those precious drops of significance for which I long so deeply. Alternatively I may choose to avoid risk-taking altogether in order to ensure I absolutely never fail. Sadly these are all manipulative tricks that I have actually used in past relationships and probably still do employ to some extent.

As we interact, you and I tend to engage in a stylised 'dance' typical of the way we uniquely relate. This can look like anything from a tango to a line-dance but is rarely like the intimate, romantic waltz of appropriate lovers. There are moves we make towards each other and moves we make to keep our distance, probably giving the appearance of intimacy while never actually moving in harmony face to face. If I have an internalised hope that you will come through for me, then I will risk moving towards you to get. If I have no internal hope that you will come up with the goods, despite my best efforts at manipulation, I will retreat and keep you at a distance, nursing anger and disappointment. Then either I minimise and bury my need or else fill it with things rather than people (possessions, fantasy life, food, television, shopping and so on).

My part in the dance (what I do to move towards you to get for myself and what I do to move away to protect myself) is my self-centred, individual style of relating. Others perceive my relational style and experience the consequences of it, but I rarely see it myself. The same is true of you. Usually you and I unconsciously employ different relational styles with different kinds of people. I might be dominant and controlling with children, meek and submissive with authority figures, promiscuous with men, distant and cold with women. It all depends what I have decided I need to get from whom. My relational style is the blanket of fig leaves I put on to cover my nakedness. It is my way of managing my world, the mask I wear, my false 'persona' as opposed to my true self. It is as if I wear a T-shirt I mostly cannot see. It shouts a statement about me to the world: *'Critic'* or *'Victim'* or *'Control-freak'* or *'Nice guy'* and so on.

Rebel   Little professor   Clown   Party animal

Rescuer   Victim   Controller/critic

Wimp   People-pleaser   Workaholic   Perfectionist

Since we all do this to a lesser or greater extent, the result is that, instead of reflecting the union of the Trinity, fallen community has become chronically broken. Not only is this because of individual independence but also because of group independence. Each recognisable family or local community or work-team or ethnic group has a 'cultural relational style', gaining its identity independently of God. We can see this operating quite clearly in the expression of national, cultural characteristics. Some of this is of God (how He intended different people groups to uniquely represent His nature) and is therefore to be celebrated. But some is community's adaptation to the fall and therefore to be repented of. Just as for individuals, the motives of independent collective culture are always mixed. Cultural relational style clearly relates to any people groups, even church groups, as much as to nations. One church community may seek to get its corporate spiritual needs met through hospitality *('We welcome therefore we are')*, another through Biblical exposition *('We know the truth therefore we are')* and yet another through slick presentation *('We're professional therefore we are')*. None of this is of God, and all of us are prone to it.

It is OK to desire that relationships offer safe attachment, mutual esteem and a sense of both individual and corporate purpose. That is what we are designed to offer each other, reflecting the parental love of God. But it is not OK to even subtly demand that others fully supply our parental need for life and personal identity. That job belongs to God. As we ignore God and take control, human relationships have been elevated as the source, rather than experienced as the enjoyable overflow.

Perfect all-providing parent – the source and sustainer

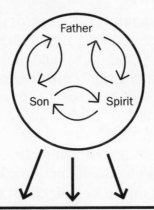

Sin = denial of dependence and declared self-dependence

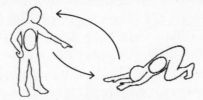

Each person *denies* dependence and *declares* independence in relation to God.
Each person *demands* in relation to others.
Each person *dominates* creation.

And so the *message* of oneness in community is corrupted and in relationship together, both individuals and people groups experience aloneness in the wider community. Difference now separates you and me through our suspicion and envy; we are unable to enjoy the wealth of diversely bearing God's image:

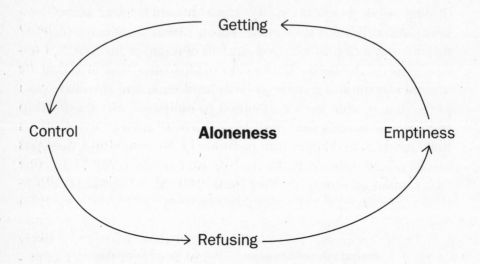

But God has told us that it is not good for us to be alone. Because of the isolation that you and I have independently created, the stewarding we offer to one another and to the planet is ineffective. We cannot rule. Without trinitarian relationship, human society fails in its role. Our work becomes nearly impossible without the network of covering and supportive unified relationships that God intends.

Thus through self-centred manipulation and self-protection, the essence of gender identity becomes radically damaged. Rather than selflessly giving myself to you, I twist the glory of masculine courage within me. Either I choose aggressive control or I retreat to non-involvement. Rather than warmly receiving into myself the good that you offer me, I desecrate the beauty of my feminine receptivity. Either I choose to wall off through stubborn refusal or I absorb everything you offer me without discrimination at all. Damaged gender identity, the delicate balance of masculine and feminine, makes for damaged sexuality. A twisted Adam and a desecrated Eve fail to relate in a way that reflects the union and harmony of the Trinity. There is no real partnership any more. The mess of human relationships we experience, whether or not they are sexualised, fundamentally emerges from the poverty we experience in our gender.

'Therefore God gave them over, in the sinful desires of their hearts to sexual impurity for the degrading of their bodies with one another. They exchanged the truth of God for a lie, and worshipped and served created things rather than the Creator...' (Rom 1:24–25).

Can I see this in my own life? In the past, when I played 'rescuer', what kind of message did I communicate to others? Certainly not *'He is therefore I am'* but something more like: *'I rescue therefore I am. (God isn't enough. I'll rescue you better than He will.).'* How did this way of relating develop? From very early on in my life, I unconsciously but firmly walled off my capacity to receive. I was always expecting sudden attack, thinking others would dump their garbage into me as if I was a landfill site. It was just easier to lock the gates twenty-four hours a day so no one could get in. Except in the rare circumstances of very safe relationships, the feminine part of my soul remained largely hidden from view.

Then, in certain controlled contexts (where I was 100% likely to offer the right kind of rescue, the right answer or the perfect performance), I found myself able to move out into the world of others. I took risks, expecting success rather than assuming failure. As a result, particularly as a woman, my gender identity was flawed. I always preferred to be the masculine giver, drawing out the receptive feminine in everyone, men and women alike, so that I could ensure I would be giving (a more powerful position) rather than receiving.

But this is not the whole story. Very rarely indeed, I would put my hope in an older woman who persistently attempted to rescue me. Typically they would not be put off by my attempts to avoid or break relationship. With a proven reduced risk of rejection, I was more prepared to receive. As their loving rescue drew out my usually well-hidden 'victim', I became hooked into a compulsive pattern of emotionally dependent behaviour where my life revolved around the other woman. Their will was my command as long as I could keep them safely connected to me. This mother and baby waltz was not always satisfying. Disappointment and rage could suddenly erupt as we stumbled about, two adults unconsciously attempting to mimic and rework a natural stage of development at a very unnatural age. But those strong emotions were always more bearable than the anxious dread I experienced at the thought of rejection. What kind of message was I communicating as I played 'victim'? Perhaps something like: *'I need help therefore I am. (God isn't enough. You'll help me better than He will.).'*

So the feminine part of me was there, I just did not get her out much. When I did allow myself to open up to another woman, my hunger for a secure place in her life seemed infinite. Once in contact with it, it was nearly impossible to close it down without compulsively absorbing the identity of the other person. Although the masculine part of me was dominant through manipulative control, the hidden feminine part of my being was clearly the most damaged. What was generating all this spoiling of the image of God within me?

CHAPTER 4
OUR ALTERNATIVE REALITY

As God tells His story in the world, He reveals that He is rational. He thinks. Being God, He has the copyright on truth. Because I look like Him, I think too. Beliefs, ideas, perceptions, imagination, dreams and intuitive understanding are all part of the incredible wealth I enjoy as I exercise my capacity to think. Like God, I also hold an individual perception of reality. I am the author of an internally held universe or frame of reference that may or may not agree with yours or His in every detail. This internal and possibly alternative reality forms the basis of my life experience. I live my life and express my story according to my own frame of reference and not necessarily according to what is objectively true.

Exchanging the truth of God for a lie

When I consider the messiness of life, I find myself blaming my poor choices on either my feelings or my circumstances: *'If I didn't feel so bad, I would get up earlier.'* *'If I had a better income, I would be more sociable.'* At times I desperately seek a change in my feelings or my circumstances to bring about the required transformation towards a happy, satisfying life.

At times like that I try to remember that the apostle Paul has bluntly told me that personal change comes through the renewing of my mind. In other words I have to look at changing my thinking, rather than my feelings or my circumstances. And of course the particular transformation Paul has in mind is radical Christ-like change from the inside out, which may or may not include me being happy. To be honest, most of the time I am still looking for instant comfort rather than radical heart surgery. I want short-term gain to reduce the impact of my long-term pain. But Paul seems to be challenging me to become recognisably different to non-members of God's kingdom. If I am to take this seriously, I need to understand the mechanics of my thinking from God's point of view.

What does Scripture have to say about this psychological

process? It seems to indicate that my thinking is the foundation of my soul. As we have seen before, one clear example describing the links between thinking, emotion and choice is found in Adam's changing perception of self: *'I was afraid because I was naked; so I hid'* (Gen 3:10). The experience of hearing God walk through the Garden passed through the filter of Adam's perception ('I am not OK because God is not OK') and he felt fear. He made an independent choice to manage this uncomfortable emotion. He hid behind a tree.

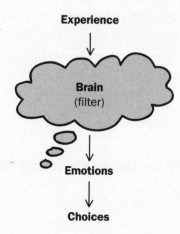

What about a more modern example? Suppose I am standing on a crowded escalator at Christmas, gripping bundles of shopping. I am tired. My brain has switched off from everything around me and is now entertaining the perennial problem of finding a present for Grandma. I want to give her a different present from last year. What do I get a woman who is eighty-five years old and has everything? Meanwhile something is tapping repeatedly on the side of my ankle: *'tap – tap – tap'*. In the crush of people, I find that I cannot turn around to discover its source.

How do I feel? Irritated, angry? What do I feel like doing with that emotion? Likely as not, whatever the difficulties of the environment, I might turn around, thinking I could communicate my dissatisfaction through the look I give. Now, what or whom do I imagine is battering at my ankle? Maybe my mind conjures up a small boy with a new toy, testing out its strength against the fragility of my bone structure? I might think of what I am going to say or how I am going to glare as I turn my head and see... a partially sighted man persistently tapping his white stick between the side of the escalator and my ankle. He is clearly attempting to pre-emptively 'see' the end of the escalator so that he can alight without accident to himself, me or others.

Suddenly my perception of the situation has radically altered. What I believed was a deliberate or thoughtless action against me, I now see as normal and good given the circumstances. Instantly my irritation melts. How do I feel now? Likely as not I experience a degree of embarrassment at my initial reaction, some compassion for the man and a desire to oversee or enable his manoeuvring off the escalator so that he comes to no harm. This is a totally different relational communication to a glaring look.

Clearly my feelings and choices emerge, not because of the circumstantial events of my life, but through my deeply held beliefs and perceptions of those events. This is the ABC theory of emotion:

A = an experience
B = my underlying belief about **A**
C = my subsequent emotion and consequent behaviour
C is caused by B, not A

So how has independence affected my thinking? Once again Paul is blunt in the early part of his letter to the Romans. Here is my own version of that passage (Romans 1:20–25): *'Since the beginning I have been clearly visible (just look at what I have made!) so you have no excuse... and although you really do know Me, you refuse to recognise me for who I am or depend on Me as you should because your thinking has become useless and your undiscerning heart (the very centre of your thinking, choosing and feeling) has become darkened: covered, concealed and obscured from the light. Though you claim to understand, actually you have become stupid and have given up relationship with Me, your Creator, to get your needs met by bits of creation – ashes and dust that I hold together and that can't even exist without Me!*

So I'm letting you eat the fruit of what you've chosen. You've dumped Me and My reality and gone and sat yourself down in an alternative universe, where you relentlessly pursue the god you think will do the trick rather than the real thing – Me.'

In other words my thinking is rather like an iceberg floating in a glassy, black sea where no sunlight penetrates. Most of the active substance has become obscured and is beyond current, conscious awareness:

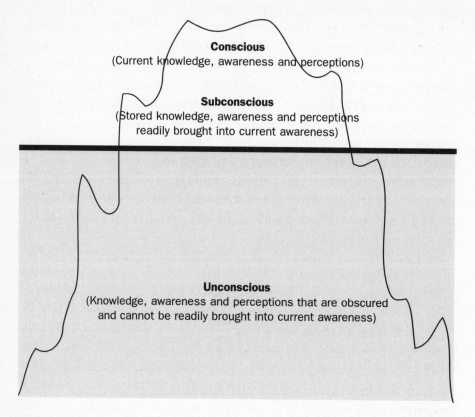

Conscious
(Current knowledge, awareness and perceptions)

Subconscious
(Stored knowledge, awareness and perceptions readily brought into current awareness)

Unconscious
(Knowledge, awareness and perceptions that are obscured and cannot be readily brought into current awareness)

For example, what were you thinking about just before you started to read this question? Maybe you were aware of reading the text and were forming beliefs and opinions about the content and concepts. Or perhaps you were thinking about chocolate biscuits, or how loud the radio is from the flat next door. Your mind may well have disconnected quite often from the words you read on the printed page, so that your conscious awareness had absolutely nothing to do with your current activity. Rather like driving a car on automatic pilot, this dissociation is very normal and is one way we defend ourselves from the rawness or monotony of fallen existence.

Likewise, what am I actually thinking about? I am aware of typing at a keyboard. I am thinking about the pain in my back caused by poor posture. I am also simultaneously daydreaming about how pleasant it would be to sit in the sun-drenched conservatory and drink coffee instead. This is my conscious thinking. But at any moment, I can tap into my subconscious thinking and offer information about my address, what colour I like best, what I think of opera or Shakespeare, a few memories of childhood or thoughts of last week. The subconscious is that area of my thinking, awareness, memory and beliefs that I can focus on currently if I choose.

But my unconscious is rather different. It includes memories, knowledge, perceptions, awareness and beliefs that are all a real part of me but cannot be brought readily into current awareness by simply willing that it be so. Some of this is trivia that is readily forgotten: what I had for breakfast on 21 February 1989, or the fish gill diagram I had to memorise for a biology exam when I was fifteen. But some of my unconscious material is composed of vital memories and underlying perceptions about myself and others. Without realising it, most of my life is routinely hidden and stored in this way. In an attempt to dull the pain of independence, at some deep level I choose to make myself only superficially aware of my existence.

As I look again at the start of Paul's letter to the Romans, it seems that prior to the fall, Adam and Eve were completely conscious. Their thinking was 'in the light' without hint of darkness or obscurity. They were fully present and alive to God, to one another and to creation without any need of dissociation. Imagine being fully sentient and sensitive to the now of existence, able to access any subconscious knowledge or memory, with all the accompanying sensory information! Before the fall, Adam and Eve knew themselves fully.

But now in the murkiness of post-fall existence, as I begin to explore my unconscious beliefs about life, the universe and everything, I see that my version of reality is nothing like God's. His thoughts really are much higher than mine. Without realising it, even as a Christian, I tend to live out of my unconscious beliefs even though these may be different to consciously professed, biblical belief. Consciously I acknowledge that God is good, but my controlling, self-centred actions give the game away and reveal that my heart holds entirely different thoughts about Him.

Like David, my heart is divided: *'Teach me your way, O Lord, and I will walk in your truth; give me an undivided heart, that I may fear your name. I will praise you, O Lord my God, with all my heart; I will glorify your name for ever'* (Ps 86:11–12).

A typical example is seen in the attitude I used to have towards criticism. Consciously my head says that in His grace and mercy towards me through Jesus Christ, God recognises me as significant and uniquely important in His kingdom, whatever I do or do not achieve, whatever mess I make. However, my heart or unconscious would say something else. Using the ABC theory:

A (an experience) = you constructively criticise a mistake in my work

C (my emotional and behavioural reaction) = I feel guilty about my mistake and ashamed of myself because you have exposed the flaw. I compulsively apologise for my existence. I try about ten times harder to make sure my work is perfect or else give up working with you altogether.

Why do I do this? What is it that I believe about you or me that makes your criticism so powerful in my life?

B (my underlying belief about A) = *'I must be perfect in every respect in your eyes, otherwise I am a failure and insignificant.'*

Believing that lie makes *you* the source of my significance, not God. But suppose I chose to dispute my underlying belief B and replace it with *'Through Christ, I am recognised as significant in God's sight whether or not I make a mistake; making a mistake is OK for a fallen, fallible human being.'* Then I might feel concerned that I may make an error, sad when I do, embarrassed when you point it out, challenged to improve my performance without killing myself, but steadfastly sure of my significance and OK-ness in God. In other words, changing my underlying beliefs at the deepest level has a profound affect on the emotions I experience when I bump into my world, and the subsequent choices I make in relationship.

Actually, mostly I no longer believe in my heart that I have to be perfect to be able to be 'seen' without shame. God has brought radical change to my life. This means that, rather than protect myself in the shadows of obscurity, I am able to take the risk of engaging in the workplace in a way I have never done before. However, having emerged from perfectionism I see that then I started to play a different game. This exposed another underlying belief: *'To be recognised as significant by you, I must prove myself bet-*

ter at my particular profession than my peers.' Transformation through the renewing of the mind is clearly a slow process! I was still dogged by a competitive attitude to work that was only a marginal improvement on perfectionism. At least I was willing to involve myself and expose my professional practice to others. But the competitive relational style emerging from my thinking was self-centred, personally stressful and, at times, refused to celebrate the unique gifting of others.

I need to make my unconscious beliefs conscious, because then, with God's help, I can renew my thinking. But how do I discover those unconscious beliefs? Daydreaming, night dreaming and fantasies are common mechanisms that I use to cut myself off from conscious reality and to unearth and process unconscious material. As I am willing to explore these under the guidance of the Holy Spirit and with the help of others, I become more aware of my underlying beliefs and strategies for independent survival. Likewise journalling my thoughts as a continuous stream provides me with a wealth of similar information. In all this exploration, I begin to see that my unconscious thinking is often very irrational. It is full of demands, catastrophic thinking and judgemental generalisations: *'I must be good in order to be loveable'*; *'If you reject me I won't survive'*; *'Being alone with you is dangerous'*.

But where do these beliefs and perceptions come from? Where did I learn that I was not OK? In fact, God asked Adam the very same thing: *'Who told you that you were naked?'* (needy and impoverished). Like Adam and Eve, the beliefs I hold are influenced by God, the enemy, my own fallen nature and by others. In different ways, God is constantly communicating His worldview to me, which the enemy attempts to twist through my experience of both nature and nurture.

For example, because of my mother's own mental health problems, I may have a biological pre-disposition to paranoid thinking. Likewise, the balance of hormones that flooded her womb when I was a tiny foetus will have profoundly influenced whether I think in a more masculine, solution-focused manner or in a more feminine, relationally-based way. Clearly this is likely to impact whether I see myself as more masculine or more feminine, independent of my actual gender as God sees it, and independent of the nurturing I receive. These are just some of the ways in which nature has impacted my thinking, without me even realising it.

Alongside this, as I am continually nurtured through my life-experience and my cultural environment, I form deeply held beliefs and perceptions by 'listening' to both truth and lies. Truth is offered by God either directly or as He reveals himself in creation. Deception is offered by the evil one, both directly and through the repeated impact of fallenness in creation. I 'listen' chiefly through observation of significant people and my experience of hurts and successes in life, particularly in my early years when my mind is more easily conditioned. As I 'listen', I formulate unconscious conclusions about God, myself and the nature of relationship.

For example, my parents and the extended social structure of childhood may give me complex, mixed messages. On the one hand, the fact that parents stay together in covenant relationship sends me a message of God's commitment to His people, His grace, patience and loyalty through adversity. On the other hand, maybe parental outbursts of anger speak of a judgemental care-giver who suddenly imposes undeserved punishment. Such messages do not describe the perfect parenting of God.

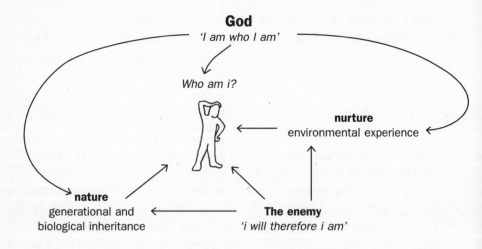

The quality of the message I receive depends largely upon the message life gives me through both nature and nurture, but also upon how I twist that message as I receive it, usually in my attempt to make sense of a very confusing universe. A clear example of an irrational perspective that can seem rational is found among those who have been sexually abused as children. Unconsciously they may see the abuse as tolerable if it meant they got a cuddle instead of the usual neglect. Rationally, sexual abuse is not tolerable, but it would seem so to you and me if that were the only way we were likely to be 'loved'.

For myself, at each moment of my life, I have inherited, absorbed and created distorted perceptions. Outside the gracious action of the Holy Spirit, I do not and cannot see straight. Yet in Christ the power of the resurrection is available to me to renew wrong thinking that has arisen from either nature or nurture. God literally intends me to be a new creation in every way.

Sadly I realise that most of the time I still 'see' myself, others and relationship through the 'lenses' I have mostly inherited or developed as a child. My image-bearing gives me the potential to 'see' perfectly as God does. But being conceived into a fallen world and suffering the blight of original sin is like being forced to wear a pair of thick, darkly tinted glasses. What do I see then? A blur of fuzzy shapes looming and diminishing. Wearing these glasses, year after year, means that my eyes and brain have been conditioned to rely on them. My stumbling actions as an adult expose the fact that although my spiritual 'eyes' are potentially perfect, the conditioning of my brain is such that I can no longer 'see' clearly beyond my nose and have not been able to for years.

I sometimes imagine that coming into human existence and entering a fallen world is a lot like that. God has set eternity deep within my heart. Hidden below the dross of the fall, I do have the bright memory of Him and His version of reality. At some very deep level this is the version of reality I hope for. But the eyes of my heart see only the same hints and shadows I have been gazing at for a lifetime. Outside the gracious intervention of God, I view a very different picture from the one He intended. As I perceived my father, brothers, male teachers etc, so in my adult life, I tend to see men and Father God. As I perceived my mother, sisters, female teachers etc, so in my adult life, I tend to see women and the maternal heart of God. Fundamentally, like Adam and Eve before me, I have listened to and unconsciously believed the deception: God is fallen, somewhat self-centred and certainly not up to the job of parenting me anywhere near perfectly.

Dependent upon... ?

So my thinking determines my choices, even the most fundamental choice of how to satisfy my parental needs – the spiritual thirst at the core of my being. God does not need me, yet He passionately longs that I might know Him, be with Him and intimately enjoy Him for ever. To image and match His own longing, God has carefully crafted my dependency in my parental needs. Although I may well ordinarily be quite unaware of it, I passionately yearn to know Him as God and experience myself as His. But because, like every other fallen human being, I unconsciously doubt the absolute goodness of any parental figure, I have made hidden choices to be independent rather than dependent in this type of relationship. Consequently my unsatisfied needs drive me to find other sources of 'life' upon which I unconsciously depend for my personal identity. Just as when He asked Adam and Eve, so God turns my attention to the fundamental problem of independence: *'What is this you have done?'*

How have I decided upon these other sources of life? From both nurture and nature and my consequent distorted perceptions about reality, I have formed an unconscious core belief about what will satisfy my longing for identity. Whatever the source, the positive experiences of my life have tended to confirm how to ensure my needs are met. Likewise the negative experiences have tended to confirm how to protect myself from unmet need. Whatever the initial and foundational impact of nature, the impact of nurture is also worth exploring thoroughly because of the repeated behavioural conditioning that it offers.

For example, when life has gone well for me in the past, I may use those memories to comfort myself in the present. Probably the memories I use have a theme: being held and connected to another, being valued enough by others as they provide for me, being seen as special and unique. I need to start asking myself some really searching questions:

What do I really long for in relationship?

When and with whom have I been even conditionally secure in relationship, sufficiently valued to be well provided for and recognised as significant? At those times, what did I learn about how to achieve that? What am I still doing to get relationship to work for me?

I long for acceptance. From my perspective, this longing was finally, conditionally satisfied in relationship with my mother. As an older child, I seemed to become her rescuer, learning that I could safely attach to her through providing the emotional support she desperately needed through prolonged mental and physical illness. Thus my rescuing relational style was created, based on the life script: *'I save you therefore I am.'* Another of my longings is to be seen as significant. A few positive memories about achieving recognised success tumble from my mind. Rarely now, I still catch myself comforting my empty spirit with a fantasy of being acclaimed before others. Internally I am still hungry to be seen and affirmed. As a child, I drank the sweet liquor of the positive recognition of others every time I worked hard or came out top of the class. These are the real 'ups' of my childhood life experience, and how I milked that source of conditional significance! Thus the workaholic 'little professor' relational style was created, based on the life script: *'I am seen as the best therefore I am.'*

Why did I need this? Why did I not believe that I was OK independent of failure or lack of recognition? I need to look at the other part of my childhood experience for this – the 'downs':

What are the big disappointments in my life? Can I feel the associated pain that still reverberates as a result? What did I learn at those times? What am I still doing in relationship to avoid ever feeling similar pain again?

I see that some of my big disappointments are about not being noticed and therefore not valued or accepted in relationship. From my perspective, some painful issues in my life seemed overlooked by both myself and others. It is as if some aspects of me were invisible and therefore neglected. The pain of perceived neglect is often more difficult to grasp than abuse. (Remarkably, at least abuse involves focus and contact in relationship.) Can I feel the pain of apparent invisibility? From my perspective, it seems to colour my childhood experience with a dull and almost imperceptible grey. That background hue only becomes visible when I consider the colourful household of a childhood friend, like the contrast between thin gruel and a bright birthday cake with candles. Amid what I perceived as absence of relationship, I took on the belief that I was unseen and unwelcome to others. To avoid the consequent pain and reduce my confusion, I tended to keep my distance. Rather than risk intimacy, feel my thirst and have no one offer to provide, I preferred to be seen only when I could ensure I was needed or could give a 'best' or 'perfect' performance. My unconscious childhood relational style clearly made my position even worse. The consequence for me as an adult is that there have been many relationships and public situations in which I have unconsciously hung back through fear of rejection.

Thus a relational style, initially inherited through fallen genetic characteristics, was confirmed and perfected: a moving towards others through rescuing or 'best' performance (when I have hope for acceptance, worth and respect), and a moving away through hiding in the crowd (when I have no hope for acceptance, worth or respect). My deep needs in relationship are legitimate. It is what I do to meet those needs which gets me into trouble and in no way communicates the *message* of a compassionate and gracious God.

CHAPTER 5
REAL NEEDS – REAL DEMANDS

In his letter to the Philippians, the apostle Paul describes the process of becoming like Christ. First he faces and honours who he was and how his upbringing, race and culture have shaped him. Then he counts it all as rubbish in order to become a child of God rather than simply the product of his ancestors and his life experience. In other words, no amount of excellent racial, cultural or parental conditioning can compare with the perfect inheritance and parenting of almighty God.

In the same way, I need to fully acknowledge my old self, made in the image of the nature and nurture I received, in order to put it to death completely. Because my thinking is core to who I become, I need to carefully explore both my rational inheritance and my mental conditioning, both godly and ungodly. Much like everyone else, life has offered me some very mixed messages about parental love, and in my own way I have also mixed the messages I received. When I 'hear' the truth, sometimes I believe it, other times I twist it. When I 'hear' a lie about love, sometimes I believe it and other times, by the grace of God, I remain in the truth. So, as a Christian, the fruit I offer others is a hybrid, tasting just as much of independence as of the Spirit.

As I look back at my childhood and my own biological, racial and cultural inheritance, I face the possibility of two equal and opposite errors. Each is worth avoiding and typically I might swing from one to another until I finally find real objectivity in Christ. Sometimes I defensively uphold those responsible for my nature and nurture as the next thing to God incarnate, at other times I bin them as totally bad. For example, I seem to have inherited a 'white protestant work ethic' from previous generations of border English/Scots. Because that perspective has seemingly helped me to survive then foolishly I tend to believe it is correct and may seek to promote that perspective. However, if that standpoint had significantly harmed me then I would tend to be prejudiced against a strong work ethic and bin both the people and cultures that promote it. Neither reaction is what the apostle Paul chooses. Instead he carefully honours his own experience of 'the flesh' (nature and nurture) for what it is, good in part but nevertheless imperfect and therefore unworthy of his confidence in comparison to being found as a new creation in Christ. This is my task ahead, to follow the same discipleship road.

Yet another pitfall on this journey will be the temptation to focus on my own parenting skills rather than my experience of being parented. It is really helpful to examine how well or how poorly I parent – whether my own kids, my Sunday school class, less experienced Christians, my counselling clients, etc. But, as an adult in Christ, I will parent others well and appropriately when I stop attempting to resolve my own childhood through their lives. Mostly, people have a hard enough time living their own lives without having to live mine as well.

Childhood needs

If I want to explore the conditioning of my thinking, I need to determine when that conditioning starts. From what tender age am I able to hold a rational perception? King David makes the biblical position quite clear: *'Surely I was sinful at birth, sinful from the time my mother conceived me. Surely you desire truth in the inner parts; you teach me wisdom in the inmost place'* (Ps 51:5–6).

David is speaking about his ability to choose independence (and therefore to perceive God) from the moment he was conceived. How can a one-celled human being desire, perceive, choose and feel, when it has no organised brain? I wonder sometimes if our spirits and souls are less confined to our grey matter than we think. Scientifically documented, post-trauma, out-of-body experience confirms that people seem to be able to perceive independently of the flesh. Like David, I believe that a one-celled human being is not just a person in potential but is in fact gloriously made in the complex image of God, amid unsophisticated flesh. Why should I not be able to desire, perceive, choose and feel (albeit in simplistic 'binary' terms such as trust or mistrust, presence or absence, yes or no, joy or despair)? Essentially David reminds me that from conception I have a legitimate spiritual parental need for unconditional love, and I can choose how to meet that need.

Like any other child, as I developed in this fallen world God clearly intended that two people enjoy the awesome responsibility of overseeing and ensuring the welcome, provision and recognition I so critically needed. Whatever the position later on in childhood, every human being is naturally designed to develop in the context of the union of a man and a woman, a father and a mother. From the beginning of my existence, God allowed me to enter their fallen and messy world, helplessly dependent upon them as physical parental figures. Does He do this to cruelly subject me to a childhood of pain and disappointment amid fallen family relationships? I think not. Although for some of us, that is how it can seem.

In part, my coming into being was an invitation from almighty God to my genetic parents. Through my arrival into their lives, He was asking if they would grasp this opportunity to depend upon Him and communicate to me His profound message of unconditional love. But mum and dad were not the only ones to get the invitation, I was being invited too. As my parental needs were met or neglected (even accidentally) by human beings, would I nevertheless seek to receive the good that my parents offered? Would I honour that in some ways they looked like God? In spite of my losses and inherited weaknesses, would I then choose to trust God as He is and live a purposeful existence, carried by Him in this fallen world? *'Listen to me... you whom I have upheld since you were conceived, and have carried since your birth. Even to your old age and grey hairs: I am he, I am he who will sustain you. I have made you and will carry you; I will sustain you and I will rescue you'* (Is 46:3–4).

The development of security – the message of attachment

At the earliest stages of human development, a person has few individual boundaries. Utterly receptive, we function almost entirely in the feminine, soaking up everything in our environment like a sponge. Our initial life-script is one of complete dependence upon our environment: *'As I experience my world, so I am.'*

Now without the gracious intervention of the Holy Spirit, I am not likely to recall what it was like to be a one-celled being. But perhaps I can begin to consider what it was like to enter the world for the first time by imagining what it is like to look for my first job. As I arrive at the interview, I am hoping for acceptance. I question whether or not there is a place for me there. Sometimes consciously, sometimes unconsciously, I wonder to myself: *'Do they want me? When they see me, will they accept me? Will I fit in?'*

In the same way, as I actually entered the world I needed a place in the lives of others where I could be in relationship. Within my extended family, within my cultural, racial and social system, I hoped that I was wanted. Supported by these wider systems, together my mother and father were given the responsibility to welcome and accept me into the world. Initially my mother's womb then her loving embrace and even later the family relational structure in the home were meant to offer an unconditionally safe, boundaried, nurturing container. In these places I needed to experience *safe attachment* at the centre of parents' welcoming, positive and reassuring attention.

Relationship with our mother is rather unique in that she is literally the doorway to others. Within her womb or later face to face, as I soaked up the security of her unconditional love, I had the potential to gain a solid sense of existence as a human being: *'Because I am safely attached, I am secure and can come into existence.'*

In many ways, as a young infant, my initial identity would naturally be that of my mother. Being the centre of my own universe, I would see her as an extension of myself. She was my place. Umbilical connection and breastfeeding were designed to offer intensely pleasurable experiences – a sense of deep connection and 'oneness' with the source of life. Ideally, this would produce a whole-body response of relaxation and contentment in me as an infant, laying down images of the joy of connectedness with another, preparing me for intimacy with others and with God.

In my developing sense of security, my father was by no

means redundant. He was invited to communicate his welcome and unconditional acceptance to me in two ways. First, like my mother, I needed him to lovingly connect with me, both through my mother's body as I grew in the womb (calling me out into face-to-face relationship) and then directly. At every stage I needed both my parents to oversee my security: to provide or ensure that I found my place in my environment with safe connection and acceptance from others who would care well. This applied as much to protecting me as the newborn in their arms as to (more tentatively) overseeing the leaving and cleaving process of my marriage or my entry into the world of adult employment, as well as everything in between. Secondly, I needed my father to unconditionally accept and protect my mother and the family system, welcoming the changes faced during pregnancy, childbirth and beyond into child rearing. For me to experience security from my father, I needed my mother and family to experience security in him – for him to accept the whole package of my existence and its impact upon his life.

The development of self–worth – the message of provision

Suppose I am accepted for that first job. On my very first day at work, I am given my desk and my place in the company. Since everything is new to me, there is much that I need from my employers. Sometimes consciously and sometimes unconsciously, I wonder to myself: *'Will I get the help I need to make a go of this?'* In the same way, as a developing child, if I had found my safe, connected place in the lives of others, I would need unconditional loving provision to develop.

I needed my parents to be unreservedly resourced by my extended family, my cultural, racial and social systems. Out of that wider resourcing, I then needed my parents to provide for me physically, psychologically and spiritually within each stage of my development. I also needed them to oversee that provision in other contexts (school, other care-givers, peers, etc.), ensuring it was sufficient. The provision I actually needed was diverse: food, clothing, a home, emotional support, affirmation, challenge, boundaries for behaviour, knowledge of the world, stimulation to learn, siblings, friendship, appropriate play, spiritual direction and so on. I would experience my value through the nuclear family, the extended family, school, church, social networking etc. as I saw folk selflessly putting themselves out to meet my needs. Thus I would have the potential to gain both well-being and hope for personal development: *'Because I am provided for, I am valuable and can become myself'*.

The development of significance – the message of respect

Suppose that first job has now become the one I have been doing for the last two years. The probationary period is long over and I am well settled into the routine. Having enjoyed and overcome the initial challenges, I am probably functioning adequately in my role and so my needs are changing. I need someone to 'see' me, to recognise and affirm my abilities, my unique role and my particular successes. I also need some direction and guidance about how to develop, how to move on to the new challenges that lie ahead. Sometimes consciously and sometimes unconsciously, I wonder to myself: *'What exactly am I here for? Where am I going next?'*

In the same way, as a developing child, if I had found a safe place to be and was filled up with all that I needed in order to become, I would now need to know what I was here for and how to move on to the next stage.

As a toddler and again as an adolescent, I would begin to develop individuality as I was allowed to discover my will and form my own boundaries. Prior to being a toddler, my boundary would have been essentially my mother. From that place of safety, I would hope to venture out, discovering that which is beyond her: my father, my siblings and so on. Now my mother's enclosing nur-

turing circle would need to gradually release me with her blessing, as I began to make my own choices in the light of her acceptance and esteem. Again, prior to adolescence, my boundary was essentially my family, then I hoped to venture out to discover that which was beyond the family: peers, social systems, adult culture and so on. Within adolescence, there would probably be a little reworking of the very early stages of my childhood: am I secure, valuable and significant? Will you love me however badly I behave according to your boundaries? Is love unconditionally based upon grace rather than conditionally based upon your law? At this time, ideally the family nurturing circle would allow me to gradually leave with blessing, as I began to make my own choices in the light of unconditional parental acceptance, provision and respect.

I would need my extended family, my cultural, racial and social systems to enable both my parents and myself in this important transition. As I left either my mother's or the family's nurturing circle, I would need the masculine in each parent and particularly my father to provide individual direction for me. As I responded to his affirming, respecting and guiding voice, he would call me out of the nurturing circle and into the welcoming world beyond. As I experienced his respect and belief in me as uniquely significant (and separate from my mother), I would have the potential to gain status, a sense of my individual identity (both as a purposeful person and in my gender): *'Because my father recognises my unique significance in who I am as a boy or girl, I am significant and I can be myself.'*

Becoming a person

This developmental journey seems to have been designed by God to be punctuated by cycles of change and rest. A change of *place* (womb, mother, family, home, school, job etc) offers oppportunity to learn to give of myself. I move out towards others, experience a receptive welcome, connect with them and initially impact their lives. Rest follows change and offers opportunity to learn to receive from others. As I am accepted I remain, receive adequate provision and mature to a wholeness appropriate to that stage. I am then called forward towards further change (moving on to the next *place* in my developmental journey). I need to be supported in that process. In this way I continually learn the fundamentals of relationship, giving and receiving. This is the story I hoped for – to be wooed by the *message* into existence, into becoming and finally into being myself.

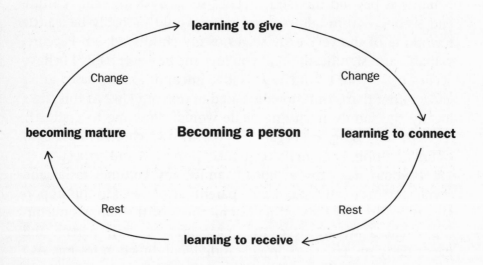

Growing demands

If that is the story I hoped for, then this is the story I got – that because of the fall I started out existence already crippled by original sin. My genetic inheritance was corrupted with the predisposition to foolish thinking and self-centred behaviour. There were physical, psychological and spiritual weaknesses as well as unresolved hurts that had passed from one generation to another, and were now ready to bear fruit once more in me.

It was not only my ability to receive that was corrupted from the start but also the ability of those around me to give. The wider family, social, national, racial and cultural systems that held my family of origin had been corrupted by the fall. Selfless service was mixed with self-interest, employment and peace with the uncertainty of redundancy and war, intelligent sensitivity with stupid indifference, affirmation and tolerance with criticism and prejudice. My potential parents found themselves inadequately 'held' and enabled by these systems, and were themselves corrupted with the same independence and mixed motives.

As a result, many of the parental needs of my childhood remained only conditionally met. Whether accidental, deliberate or circumstantial, this lack of unconditional love from others impacted me more than I then dared to admit. Sadly your story will be little different. There are many, many ways to be left hungry for love. I was separated from my mother while one of us was poorly in hospital. Maybe you were wrongly idolised and spoilt by a parent. For almost all of us, acceptance, provision and respect were only conditional on good behaviour. You may have been bullied at school, with little protection or intervention from parents and teachers. The boundaries I was offered in my teens may have been too lax. Some of us may even have experienced physical, emotional, sexual or ritualistic abuse in situations unpoliced by loving parental figures. That which parents are called to do, they sometimes fail to do; that which we hope they will not do, at times they do. Even the best motivated of even God-fearing family systems is affected by the fall, with every attitude of giver and receiver tainted by self-centred self-protection.

Whether through our refusal to receive or others' refusal to give, an unfulfilled parental need results in pain, confusion and disappointment. This pain can be experienced as overwhelming, particularly when we are young. Because infants cannot distinguish themselves much from their environment, children who experience early losses in relationship tend to become adults who feel and think in a very black-and-white way. 'Woman' triggers their anger, 'man' provokes their anxiety, everything is bad, and so on. In particular, small infants in the womb have nowhere to express the angst of the fall. Everything good or bad that their mother feels goes into them, with no means of cathartic, emotional expression. Thus repression of emotion typically begins in the womb. Infant distress, that is expressed relationally but ignored, quietens within minutes to inner despair and self-protective withdrawal. As older children we often learn to 'shut up and be good' because that is seemingly wanted by the big people in our world. From conception to adult life, the only option we believe is available may be to stuff our feelings out of sight in order to survive.

Whether selfless or selfish, the actions of others tend to be mirrored in our reactions. Every receptive and loved child becomes a giving lover. Every victim of the fall becomes an agent of sin in the lives of others because in an attempt to manage the pain and hunger of unfulfilled parental need, we are motivated to manipulate our world.

The development of insecurity – the message of detachment

Looking back on all that I legitimately hoped for, I see that significant problems in achieving a safe attachment to either my mother or father (but particularly mother) resulted in an undeveloped sense of my acceptability.

'Mummy? Daddy?'

'Am I sufficiently acceptable to say "yes" to existence?'

By a few weeks after my birth, my mother's post-natal depression had become acutely problematic, resulting in a lengthy stay in hospital, receiving electro-convulsive therapy and other treatment for her mental health. My father was literally left 'holding the baby' and decided to send me to a local nursing home for what he later regretfully called proficient, clinical professional care. Loud distress on my part resulted in the nursing home parking my pram at the bottom of their garden. Relatively speaking, I was alone with nothing to relate to but the bright blue sky of an Indian summer. My previously energetic distress quietened into rigid despair and I probably comforted myself by bonding to 'blue'. Somewhere under the vast upturned bowl of the late summer sky, I found a place. Alone and under the 'blue', I experienced safety. Away from my mother's extreme emotional reactions, isolation under the elements felt like heaven.

Years later, to avoid the anxiety provoked by insecurity, I found myself unconsciously demanding of others: *'I must securely attach to you so that I can safely exist.'* Whether the rejection I experienced was accidental or deliberate made no difference to me in my need. I found myself with a disconnected 'umbilical cord', an empty mouth seeking succour and a raging internal emptiness. With little or no sense of 'being', I was motivated to comfort myself with some kind of 'connection' and so reduce the powerful separation anxiety that I experienced. Every baby has to bond to something or someone. I had to find a place to attach. As a relatively lonely child, I would frequently lie on the lawn of my parents' garden and simply stare up into the 'blue'. As I did this, I became peaceful, at rest in my spirit. Even as an adult, I love being outside under the 'blue' and absorbing its vastness with my body, soul and spirit, preferably on the top of some high mountain where the upturned bowl can be experienced in all its magnificence.

Without realising it, I developed a relational behaviour designed either to get security (e.g. constantly seeking my mother's focused attention) or else to minimise and manage my insecurity (e.g. retreating into detachment from my mother and bonding instead with something or someone else). Fallen reactions to women and, to varying extents, all human relationship ensued. I had no real sense of a place for me to exist, no sense of 'being', and so experienced myself as 'floating' and detached in relationships. I grew up hungry for a woman's world of connected, intimate relationship, and, when I had enough hope, would draw out the feminine nurturer from others. Passing through puberty meant that I would begin to sexualise these infant longings for intimate, all-embracing connection with women. Mostly though I actually felt hopeless about connection in relationship and preferred to remain completely detached.

But that is not the entire story. It is important for me to realise the impact of nature as well as nurture. Recently I have discovered that my own experience of detachment from my mother through depressive illness is not confined to my own generation. As a young child, my mother suffered a severe detachment from my grandmother when she gave birth to twins who then died within a few weeks. Long term, my grandmother apparently became unresponsive to her family and household responsibilities. The result was that, later in my own childhood, my mother seemed to act out her own lack of mother love in relation to me. As a child, I finally but inappropriately attached to my mother through mothering and rescuing what seemed to me to be the needy child in her. Maybe this way we both got what we wanted. I got to be close to my mother and she got to be mothered. The bondage of this emotional dependency has felt extremely damaging and has impacted my relationships with women time and time again.

What I am describing here actually seems to have been a generational problem, mothers and daughters in my family tree losing early connection with one another, resulting in inappropriate emotional dependency woman to woman. For the sake of my relationship with my own children, it has been critically important to allow the blood of Christ to break the bondages in the generations and to allow these significant and painful generational losses to bleed into the wounds of Christ.

The development of worthlessness – the message of neglect

As a developing child, significant problems in gaining adequate physical, psychological or spiritual provision from my family, school, church or social system resulted in an undeveloped sense of my worth. With insufficient on offer to ensure that I could grow and develop at my own pace, I was somewhat 'stunted' and 'stuck' in my personal development.

I was a relatively lonely child both within my family, at school and among local children. Other than sitting in class, I did not enjoy the regular company of a peer my own age until I was about

'Am I sufficiently valuable to say "yes" to becoming myself?'

nine or ten years old. A busy road outside the family home, with no permission to cross it and no friends on my own side of the road meant that I usually played alone. An imaginary friend joined me regularly as we enjoyed playing tea parties in the garden. Precious, precious moments of playing with my father stand like treasured snapshots in my mind. With the loss of much childhood peer relationship, inwardly I ached without even realising it.

I had a very low expectation of family to provide and encourage friendships for me. I rapidly put no hope in those closest to me to oversee the meeting of that need because, to me, the big people in my household seemed to have their attention focused elsewhere. Seeing myself as worthless within the family system because of the lack of provision of peer relationships, I began to demand: *'You must value me enough to provide for me so that I can become myself.'*

With no sense of well-being, I needed to get self-worth from somewhere. Routinely as a child I turned to food to comfort me in that loss of companionship. Later, at university, I found myself amid thousands of peers with few social skills to access those relationships. In developing mild bulimia at that time, I was communicating my desperate need for relationship by stuffing myself with food, and also communicating my terror of engaging in relationship by voiding that same food. Out of perceived neglect, I was angry, but I had deftly turned the anger inwards towards myself. Part of my later indifference towards 'family' was no doubt an expression of the cool anger that I felt about my friendless world.

As an adult, my relational style within the larger framework of church has been described in the past as fairly shy or reticent.

Flashes of anger and outrage towards leadership would emerge on behalf of the flock, when leadership clearly failed to enable church to function as a community. When I explored this, I saw that I was, in fact, angry about what I had perceived as parental disinterest in ensuring that I had friends. I had been unconsciously using my relational style with church as a way of judging the perceived neglect in my childhood.

Again that is not the entire story, and I need to examine the impact of nature as well as nurture. Within my father's family, there seems to have been a generational problem of angry demand as the typical reaction to perceived neglect. My father's grandfather was even renowned as 'the mad John Smith' because of his temper. Again it has been vital for me to allow the blood of Christ to break any soul ties with former generations and their angry relational style.

The development of insignificance – the message of disrespect

Achieving individual significance is a complex journey. It requires both the necessary releasing from the nurturing system and a calling out into the next appropriate system (mother to family, family to peers, peers to the adult world). Either the releasing or the calling out can break down. Parents may draw a sense of identity from their role, terrified to let us go because they do not know who they are without us to nurture. Or perhaps that masculine quality, seeking to bless and call out the true self in another was not developed in either parent. They would not bless and affirm because they would not allow themselves to be blessed and affirmed in God.

For myself, problems in achieving a healthy separation from mother and in receiving recognition and direction from father resulted in an undeveloped sense of my unique purpose and gender-identity.

My father loved beauty. He readily recognised and affirmed beauty in creation: music, landscapes, people, even home furnishings. In my mind, this stands in contrast to the empty place in my spirit where I longed to be filled with his affirming comments about my appearance. Every daughter wants to be her daddy's princess, but for some reason I never heard him tell me I was his.

Father

Mother

'Am I sufficiently significant as an individual to say "yes" to being truly me?'

Whether he did offer me affirmation and somehow I refused to receive it into myself, or whether he simply did not say anything positive about my appearance remains a mystery to me.

Seeing myself as personally inadequate, and a failure as a potential woman, I began to demand of others: *'You must recognise me as uniquely significant so that I can be truly myself.'* This lack of affirmation provoked within me a deep sense of illegitimate shame. Without a sense of self, I chose to get significance through 'doing' rather than 'being'. I remember my father arriving home from a parents' evening at school and glowing with pride at my academic achievements and hard work. That night I felt he 'saw' me: my uniqueness, my gifting, energising me to draw the same kind of affirmation again. It felt so good to be 'seen' by my daddy. From that moment academic attainment became my controllable route to being 'seen', reducing the immense personal shame I held internally. Rather than face the pain of apparently not being recognised as a woman by my father, I chose instead to be recognised as an academic and a hard worker. Internally as a teenager I detached from my femininity to manage my sense of insignificance as a woman, retreating into a more transsexual view of myself and so sabotaging all routes to affirmation of my gender.

Once again I need to ask the question, what is the impact of nature as well as nurture? On my father's side at least, there is a repeated pattern through the generations of highly energetic, passionate, industrious hard workers. Please understand me, there is something of godly image-bearing in this. Yet each generation has tended to use work as an independent means to life, children learning from a parent's lap that passionate hard work will help them survive, particularly in the midst of poverty. Over the generations, the graciously given likeness of God has been twisted into a tool that we use to gain significance our own way. The passion to bring order out of chaos has so easily become corrupted into workaholism. Again I need to invite Jesus to stand between myself and my family tree. As I allow Him to absorb into Himself our idolatry of work, He continues to offer me His passion to bring order out of chaos, both directly and through the generations. Amazingly this is part of who I am as His dependent creature, the good of my inheritance as a member of my family.

Becoming alone

How has independence affected my experience of change and rest? What have I learnt in a fallen world about the fundamentals of relationship, giving and receiving? As a needy child developing a survival strategy, each disappointing experience of both change and rest motivated me to master the fundamentals of independence.

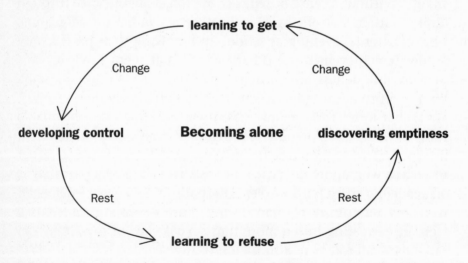

My personal boundaries and therefore gender identity would have become broken or distorted as I ceased to understand who was responsible for what. For example, my feminine capacity to receive (to say 'yes' or 'no' appropriately to another who moves into my world) could be easily wounded, particularly in very early childhood when I was most vulnerable. In order to survive in certain circumstances, perhaps I always chose to say 'yes': *'As you move into my world, in order to be acceptable to you, I will choose to receive any old junk or demands you chuck at me. I will be a 'people-pleaser', a 'good girl' or 'nice boy'. I get my needs met by keeping you happy with me.'*

Or maybe I always chose to say 'no': *'As you move into my world, in order to protect myself from disappointment, I will choose to wall up my life, hating and minimising my own neediness. In my distrust, I will refuse to receive anything from you whether you offer good or bad.'*

The masculine power to lovingly initiate (to appropriately hear and respect the 'yes' or 'no' from another as I move into their world) could be likewise frustrated or threatened in childhood. In order to survive, I may never choose to hear and respect a 'no' from another: *'As I move into your world, I am deaf to you saying "no". Disregarding your boundaries, I choose abusive control to ensure I get my needs met by you.'*

Or perhaps I choose to never hear and respect their 'yes': *'As I consider moving into your world, I am deaf to you saying "yes". I assume that you will devalue and rubbish me, so I choose to retreat to detached non-involvement, ashamed of myself, my failure and minimising my needs.'*

From early adolescence, both my childhood needs and growing demands passed through the fiery furnace of puberty. Like every other human being, my genital sexuality 'woke' up fully and, unconsciously, I tended to sexualise my parental needs. In other words I began to use a tool, designed specifically to fulfil my peer needs, to satisfy the parental needs instead. Because of the differences in how crucial these two types of need are, this was a little like holding a friend's hand in a desert in order to keep myself alive. What I actually needed was water not companionship.

Admittedly it is not good for human beings to be alone, but without fulfilled parental needs, you and I will simply die. One set of needs is important, the other is crucial to survival. My demands for safe physical attachment, attention, and recognition of my adequacy as a person tend to become fused with my genital reactions. Likely as not, I probably absorbed the cultural deceit that the purpose of sex is for giving pleasure to myself rather than appropriately blessing and giving pleasure to another: *'If you do not sexually fulfil me, I have grounds to break the relationship'*, or, *'I have a right to genital intimacy according to my perceived preference'* and so on.

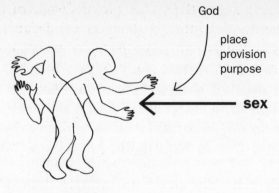

God

place
provision
purpose

← **sex**

Parental needs

The gift of sex is intended as an intimate expression of the *message* between a man and a woman in a covenant relationship before God: *'For this reason a man will leave his father and mother and be united to his wife, and the two will become one flesh. This is a profound mystery – but I am talking about Christ and the church'* (Eph 5:31–32).

Within God's economy, sex is about selflessly blessing rather than getting, and warmly receiving rather than protecting myself. The wider impact of godly sexual union within marriage is immense. This glorious but rather private message is more publicly proclaimed through the relational health of a covenanted marriage, within our family, social and working life. Once we let God proclaim the *message* in the privacy of the marriage bed, trinitarian love spills out into every part of the fabric of society.

Independence has marred the dignity of sexuality. Ungodly family norms about gender, bodies, sexual development and the preciousness and exclusivity of marriage lay down unhelpful symbols in our thinking. Sexuality and gender identity may be damaged through inappropriate contact with either sex. For some children, this may provide the only source of intimacy. The resultant distortion in our perception of sex, gender, bodies and intimacy is profound. Some of us may use masturbation as a 'pacifier' in anxious situations. As we observe the dysfunctional 'relational dance' between our parents, we tend to adopt similar practices as we relate to both the opposite and the same sex. We may even unconsciously choose sexual partners with similar relational styles to parents because we have already learnt how to manage that gender to get what we need parentally. Inappropriate erotic attachments or angry detachments from either sex may occur.

For some of us the launch into the world of adult relationships is coloured with confusion about our gender and the nature of true intimacy. Our pattern of relating at a sexual level can become a major part of our strategy for survival. Most sexual problems highlight an underlying struggle to avoid true intimacy. As we unconsciously sexually demand secure love, self-worth and significance, each idolatrous relationship (fantasy, reality or even our spouse) ties us wrongly to another human being. We may walk through our adult lives never having truly left home, uniting ourselves intimately and sometimes sexually to all and sundry with the resultant spiritual ties. Consequently we find ourselves unable to cleave appropriately in ordinary friendship or to a marriage partner.

Active sexual compulsion is typically satisfied when we fulfil our parental needs by relating purely at the level of orgasm or fantasy. The erotic 'rush' can emotionally and chemically hook us, so that we behave like junkies and slip down into the secret realm of sexual addiction, which may be a life-long struggle. Frigidity on the other hand is the lack of capacity to feel or respond erotically in appropriate situations. It is often about minimising legitimate parental needs, detaching in relationship and inappropriate symbolising of gender identity, sex and marriage. While sometimes tolerated within Christian marriage, frigidity can indicate a more significant level of independence than sexual compulsion. Sadly, the church often judges the problems the other way around.

Like a number of other teenagers, whether male or female, passing through puberty meant that both my unmet needs for affirmation from a father and the acceptance of a mother could be sexualised. Without realising what was happening, I began to relate sexually to men in ways that managed my hunger for affirmation from my father. However, I also found myself attracted to some women to gain a fundamental acceptance of me as a person. And so fallen heterosexuality and nurture-based homosexuality developed within me, alongside one another. (The same kind of problems can occur with men relating sexually to either women or other men in an effort to manage their unmet maternal or paternal needs.) Again, when I look at my family tree it seems inevitable that biology and generational inheritance have also played their part here.

While all along there is the story that I had hoped for and the story that I got, the awful truth is that mostly I still find myself living the story that I choose, preferring an impoverished diet under my control, often refusing the blessing that others may offer simply because it is not all that I had precisely hoped for. And what difference would it have made if at those critical moments in my life I had turned and listened to God and allowed Him to sustain me? He says He has upheld me since I was conceived, and has carried me since my birth. He says He still continues to sustain me and rescue me. He also says that I am without excuse in any apparent ignorance because, whether or not I knew Him personally at the time, He has constantly whispered His presence to me through all that He has created.

As I think on that I see that the truth is that in every moment of my life He was there to lean upon. He was there to attach to as a mother when mine had gone. He was there to befriend me and play with me when I was alone. He was there telling me I was beautiful when there were no human words heard. He was there absorbing the bentness of my generational inheritance and yet still offering me the good of it. He was there that I might be a completely new creation in Him. The truth is that rather than trust Him and risk confirming He was just as disappointing as everyone else, I would rather manage life my own way. A victim of a fallen world, the child I was became an agent of sin in the lives of others, using them to my own ends, getting them to parent me through my sinful relational style. Hiding within my teenage and now adult body, this child sometimes still moves towards others to 'get'. At other times she avoids involvement, protecting herself from disappointment. In this I am demanding that others, not God, must meet my crucial parental needs. My self-determined, controllable life-sources or 'broken cisterns' displace God from His rightful position as provider: *'You shall have no other gods before me. You shall not make for yourself an idol in the form of anything in heaven above or on the earth beneath or in the waters below. You shall not bow down to them or worship them; for I, the LORD your God, am a jealous God'* (Ex 20:3–5).

CHAPTER 6
THE REALITY OF THE CROSS (I)

We are half-hearted creatures, fooling about with drink and sex and ambition when infinite joy is offered us, like an ignorant child who wants to go on making mud pies in a slum because he cannot imagine what is meant by the offer of a holiday at the sea. We are far too easily pleased.[4]

C.S.Lewis

Lewis is right. This child within me is so stupefied by the fall that she cannot conceive of her parental hunger being completely satisfied by someone unseen. Instead she prefers to mildly assuage that hunger herself with what is tangible, known but impoverished, rather than risk being disappointed again.

I think that my bid for independence through 'making mud pies in a slum' has been most clearly seen in my search for safety. Like many women, I have often used control to manage my raging thirst for a secure place in the life of another. Men, on the other hand, more typically thirst for recognition and purpose through their work. As you read on, gentlemen, perhaps you may find it helpful to replace words like 'safety' and 'connection' with something more suitable for you, maybe 'purpose' and 'respect'?

God wants me to quench my thirst through relationship with Him rather than manipulating others into keeping me safely attached to them. If I were to tune in to God's story in my life, I would discover that He has often whispered to me about these two sources of spiritual provision: Himself and everything else. He has wanted me to see and feel the difference, so that I could choose for myself whom I will serve. For example, in order to help me God has often seemed to harm me by allowing my sources of safety to dry up. On good days, when I have felt my thirst I have come running back to Him. Sadly it is usually suffering and pain that lead me to be more dependent upon Him, like a stubborn mule that will only be governed by bit, bridle and stirrups. And as He has allowed me to suffer that thirst, so He begins to knock on the door of my heart.

Most recently God did that by allowing my daughter to suffer a potentially fatal accident. Out of my own need for safe connection in relationship, like a lot of mothers, I have probably been too controlling with my children. So when my daughter turned eighteen, carefully I spent the weekend laying her life down before God as a first fruit, releasing her into His care. The next day, far away from me in Africa, she was bitten by a deadly snake.

When the news reached me, then I felt my thirst for safety. I was split in two. The mother in me was only concerned for her daughter. But the child in me so identified with the situation that I was actually also only concerned for myself. The incident felt life-threatening to both of us.

Someone knocking at the door

'Here I am! I stand at the door and knock. If anyone hears my voice and opens the door, I will come in and eat with him, and he with me' (Rev 3:20).

Imagine the subsequent days. I listened to my daughter on the phone and heard her profound distress. After emergency medical care and by the grace of God she is still alive and remarkably has all her limbs intact. In my prayers I laid her down before God and then picked her back up, again and again and again. Why should He have her? He clearly cannot look after her properly.

What is going on here? What are the underlying beliefs governing my response? If my heart is a landscape sculpted by the beliefs I hold, I find that there are some areas that are pleasant places. Green, lush and fruitful, here God dwells and I see Him more or less as He is. Here I am His unconditionally loved child. Here I trust Him to work all things together for good as He defines it. Here I can be a good enough mother to my own child.

But I find there are other parts of that landscape of my heart: stony desert dunes where the wind moans down darkened alleys that lead to hovels fallen into disrepair. Windows and doors are firmly bolted from the inside. Here I am alone and hiding in the dark, starving and ashamed, and God looks like an enemy who wants to hurt me. Here my mothering is more about protecting me from the pain of disconnection from someone close to me than selfless love for a child. Here I have to take control and work things together for good as I define it: that my daughter stays safe, alive and thoroughly connected to me at all costs or else it will feel like I will die too. In this part of my heart I simply cannot bear life without her because unwittingly she is supplying some of my parental need for security.

Like the lukewarm Laodiceans rebuked by Jesus in Revelation, the message I offer is thoroughly mixed. The trappings of wealthy, western culture mask my spiritual poverty to such a degree that independence seems possible as a life strategy. It takes a typical, third-world, life-threatening situation to expose my profound need for security.

It is also thoroughly reasonable not to turn to a god who is fallen, a god who wants to hurt me, a god who is not good. Independence makes sense under such conditions. Which perspective about God will I choose to live out of as right and eternally true? Which perspective will be abandoned as a lie? Will I risk forsaking a view of dependency and provision that feels much more tangible because I learnt it on my parents' laps? Or do I dare become a Christian adult, and choose to take God at face value and live my life as if He actually is who He says He is? And will you dare to do the same?

When I first became a Christian, I was willing to humble myself before God and freely acknowledge what nonsense I had previously believed about Him. Now to face the foolishness of my unconscious perspective about God, I need only ask myself the radical question: *'Why do I not allow the truth about God to make a practical difference in my relationship with you?'* The answer is because, in the areas where it counts the most, I simply do not believe it. On the discipleship road, even though I may think I am outwardly a 'good enough' Christian, I need to humble myself again and again, allowing my deep doubt in God to surface and be exposed for what it is, finally dumping it as a lie. This is the process of change – being set apart from my alternative reality to be set apart into His.

Two very different perspectives, but only one absolute truth. One describes my alternative reality, the other the reality of God that I was made for. How do I move from one position to the other? Because of the impact of independence in my life, I cannot move, that is the problem. But between my personal, alternative reality (with its distorted perceptions and broken relationships) and the reality of God (with rich, satisfying involvement with others), there is a door. That door is the boundary between independence and dependence, mistrust and trust, the boundary between the desert and the pleasant places in the landscape of my heart. It is the door of the hovel in which I hide my needy, shame-filled, independent self. As Jesus knocks at the door through my life experience, He graciously asks me to invite Him into the problem. He longs to step inside, help me dismantle my independent strategy and usher in His own worldview, bring His life to me in my place of need. I do not need to move, in fact I cannot. I have only to say 'yes': *'My dove in the clefts of the rock, in the hiding-places on the mountainside, show me your face, let me hear your voice; for your voice is sweet, and your face is lovely'* (Song 2:14).

So who is this person on the other side of the door, on the outside of my hiding place? He is 'God as He is', in the flesh and on the cross, hanging there. He is the *message* through whom God the Father extravagantly and fully reveals Himself in blazing colours through the resurrected flesh of His Son. He inclines His ear as the wounded healer, ready to hear my story and literally minister through His own body to the damage within me. He is eternity breaking into time to place all my times in His hands. He has come to stand with me on my side of the infinite chasm between God and fallen humankind. With His eyes fixed upon me, He falls backwards into the hands of His Father in the most incredible trust exercise the world has ever seen. I need only walk across Him as the bridge between, because He has taken the leap of faith that I could not. In the face of the circumstances of the crucifixion that proclaimed the opposite, Jesus the perfect man has nevertheless believed in and trusted His unseen Father to be the holy and good God He always said He was.

So now I have only to look at Jesus in order to see straight about God. God has come in the flesh so that in any refusal to fix my eyes on what is unseen, I can look at what is seen instead and get the *message* right this time: *'I am the way and the truth and the life. No-one comes to the Father except through me. If you really knew me, you would know my Father as well. From now on, you do know him and have seen him'* (Jn 14:6).

The amazing grace of God is ministered to me through the cross. This is the place where the powerless become empowered, where the unable become able and the impotent become vibrantly alive. This is the place where learners become doers. This is the place where disciples are made.

This is my *place* where my fallen nature can become new creation, where my generational inheritance can become rich rather than impoverished. This is my *place*, where I can be increasingly born again into a new family with completely different ways of relating, recognising and renouncing the old and receiving the new. This is my *place* where, as a Christian adult, I can actively and energetically choose to rule over myself, taking up the authority that is now mine in Jesus Christ, claiming my new inheritance as a co-heir and co-equal with Him. He won this for me two thousand years ago. How much longer does He have to knock? He is offering it to me now. Will I take it up? Will I choose to change my mind about where life is to be found, turning from that which has taken God's place as provider in my life? Will I then turn towards God as He is, receiving His *message* through His Son Jesus Christ as He communicates a Father who is perfectly holy, good and thoroughly for me?

I cannot hope to fulfil the human calling to rule over creation until I have taken up this call to rule over myself. God will not give me more responsibility until I have begun to deal effectively with the things nearer to hand: me. This is discipleship – to first learn how to rule over myself and then to rule in practice. If the *message* is true, I had better stop messing around and get on with responding to it, learning and practising how to receive from God in order to enjoy Him as He is and glorify Him through ruling over myself and creation.

In practice, when this process of ruling takes place as an act of the will at the conscious level, it is only the very beginning of repentance. Much like the prodigal son of Luke's Gospel, I have suffered starvation far away from home. Unbelievably, this has happened through my own choices. This is the consequence of providing for myself in my own way. This is the product of instant gratification of need. Like the prodigal, I have wanted joy now rather than later. He came to his senses when he responded to the knocking at the door of his heart through the physical poverty of his circumstances. He reminded himself of his father's goodness, where real sustenance could be found. Then out of that truth he chose to go home, looking forward in faith to receiving in due time the provision that he so desperately needed. Like the prodigal, I continually need to discipline myself to call to mind that, through Jesus Christ, the truth is that the Father's attention is on me and

He loves me well whether or not I actually feel that right now. There are no conditions to this any more. Jesus has fulfilled them. When the prodigal changed his mind and started out, he had not yet enjoyed the pleasures of his father's company in the ways that he needed most; he had only reminded himself of the truth and acted upon it. That is what I need to do. My relationship with God is based on faith not my experience of what may or may not be His current dealings with humanity.

Christianity calls this spiritual discipline 'practising the presence of God'. Day by day I need to actively give up my internal struggles against God, so that He gets to be Creator and I get to be the creature. His version of reality gets to be the true and reliable one, and mine gets to be dumped. This is the true process of discipleship: ceasing to play at being a Christian and starting to grow up in Christ, living as if God is who He says He is.

There can be God-given moments in our lives when our internal perspective shifts deeply through a major turning of our will. One evening, quite a few years ago now, I lay face down on a bed exhausted and sobbing with the emerging pain of childhood years. While receiving counselling, I had come to a sudden realisation of the depth of emptiness at the core of my spirit. I knew in that moment that nothing, no woman or man, could even remotely satisfy my huge hunger for safe, perfect, unconditional love.

I realised the stark choice before me. Either I could continue to be in control of my own life, minimising my need, remaining aloof and withdrawn within relationships. I could continue to maintain the hope that somewhere there may be someone tangible who would be a 'good mother' to me, supplying what I so desperately required. Alternatively, I could choose to jump out of this place of carefully maintained safety and begin at a much deeper level to trust God in all His maternal affection towards me. I felt so tired in the desperately hard, daily work of digging my own 'broken cistern' to satisfy my spiritual thirst. Despite my best efforts, I found myself still so very thirsty. Finally, I was profoundly irritated by my unbelief. The pain and emptiness I felt was the knocking of Jesus Christ upon the door of my heart. The pain was a gift and not an enemy.

By the grace of God, I was becoming deeply motivated to shift my thinking. I had recognised an insidious belief about God as distant and cold, even malevolent towards me. Wrestling with Him in prayer, I decided purely as an act of the will to trust that God was actually as He describes Himself in Scripture: warm, loving and thoroughly for me. In that moment, it seemed to me that little of what God had done for me or allowed in my life proved the trust-worthiness of His love. At that point, I had been a Christian of one sort or another for about twenty-five years, I still didn't understand God's story in the world in sufficient depth to grasp that He was any different from anyone else. I took the only way forward and at some very deep level (yet not nearly so deep as God longed for) I rejected the version of reality that had become my familiar friend and chose to trust something entirely unfamiliar and seemingly intangible, simply because He said it was true. And out of that truth I opened the door of my heart.

It seemed to me that I took a huge risk. There were no blind-ing lights and there was no radical change in my feelings. In actively choosing relationship with God as He is, I had finally given a positive response to His insistent knocking. Jesus had just walked through a 'door' into a part of my heart that was stony with unbelief. He was about to get to work to help me dismantle my strategy of isolation and withdrawal in relationships. I could not yet see Him rolling up his sleeves, but, nevertheless, I knew He had come: *'I will remove from you your heart of stone and give you a heart of flesh'* (Ez 36:26–28).

The divine exchange

So I invite Him in. What happens next? From my real home far away, God the Father had been looking out for me. Now He scorns His own dignity, racing down the road to throw His arms around me and kiss me (in and through the cross). The best robe, the ring and the sandals are ready in His hands. Jesus, my older and more obedient brother, has not stayed at home and moaned about me to Dad. Instead, perfectly modelling His Father's love, He comes inside my hiding place. Once inside, His light reveals all. Before I had allowed Him in, the darkness was such that I could barely see the mess myself. Now He stands with me knee deep in it all, actively seeking to share in my suffering and sin. More than that, He claims that two thousand years ago this whole mess legally became His and not mine.

Perfect all-providing parent – the source and sustainer

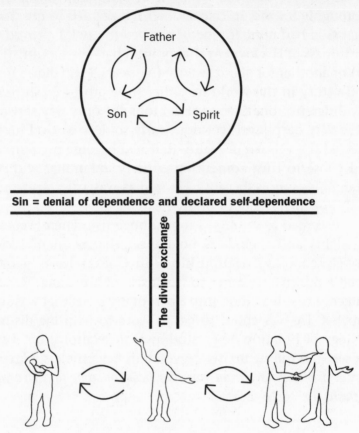

Each person has the *opportunity to receive fullness in Christ* (Col 2:10)
in relation to Father God as the source.
Each person therefore has *the ability in Christ to relate* to others
through selflessly giving and warmly receiving.
Each person has *the ability in Christ to rule* appropriately over creation.

Now I need to learn the art of letting it go, giving it to Him and, most amazing of all, agreeing that He can change places with me. He takes on my generational inheritance and I get to have His. He gets to be the baby alone without a mother, the friendless child and the unaffirmed youngster. I get to be parented by God. He gets the guilt and punishment deserved for my manipulation and withdrawal in relationships. I get to go free, righteous and unashamed, running down the road towards the arms of my Father in heaven.

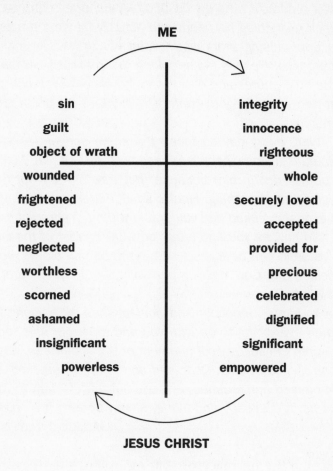

ME

sin	integrity
guilt	innocence
object of wrath	righteous
wounded	whole
frightened	securely loved
rejected	accepted
neglected	provided for
worthless	precious
scorned	celebrated
ashamed	dignified
insignificant	significant
powerless	empowered

JESUS CHRIST

Of course, I usually pretend to be outside the door, refuse to go in and assume that Jesus will sort it all out. Like most Christians, I prefer Him to change me without me having to face both the pain I feel and the pain I have caused. Mostly I have a passive relationship with the cross, but that is not God's way. Every day through one difficult circumstance after another, He invites me to actively join with Him in facing my messy independent reactions. Like the prodigal, this is where I am starving to death. It is inside my hiding place where I can joyfully discover the amazing fellowship of sharing in His sufferings, where I had unwittingly felt His pain and where He had knowingly felt mine:

He had an unpromising beginning. Like a root out of dry ground, it was a miracle he grew up at all. A vulnerable lad, he seemed to lack everything he needed to actually become a man. And to this unpromising start was added his extremely unimpressive appearance. He was plain looking, hadn't much personality and made little impression on anyone. You know, everyone reckoned that he wasn't likely to contribute much to the balance sheet of humanity.

Well, every day he faced the same dangers as you and I. Isolated and alone, people refused to really love him. No one could be bothered with him because they saw him as worthless and insignificant. A nothing. Finally, amidst intense suffering, he was left exposed, naked and vulnerable without a shred of protection.

So now as you and I look on with the rest of the crowd and we've seen him bear such heavy and painful blows, we have to conclude that God must be punishing him for some dreadful sin. But whose?

You know, innocent and unblemished as a young lamb, he carries everything to do with you and me – our sins, our suffering – into the solitary confinement of the wilderness, way outside the presence of God. Despised and rejected, stricken and smitten, pierced and crushed, and without any children to remember him, he dies silently and alone, simply bearing it all away.

(Adapted from Isaiah 53)

As I welcome the intimacy of sharing in His sufferings, the most remarkable thing happens. He stays in my hiding place and dies there and I find my home in His Father and live for ever. More than this, He comes back to life and joins me in a party with His Father. Here I can rest and make my home with Him rather than ceaselessly work to get life my own way. This is the divine exchange. The cross has already occurred. At every moment in every relationship, I can either choose to apply it to my life or not.

Choosing repentance and receiving forgiveness

When I kept silent, my bones wasted away through my groaning all day long. For day and night your hand was heavy upon me; my strength was sapped as in the heat of summer. Then I acknowl-

edged my sin to you and did not cover up my iniquity. I said, 'I will confess my transgressions to the LORD' – and you forgave the guilt of my sin. Therefore let everyone who is godly pray to you while you may be found.

(Ps 32:3–6)

There were once two men with a similar problem. Each had sinned against Jesus despite being forewarned of their sin. Although they both felt terrible about that, they each took a different route towards resolving the problem.

Perhaps in the hope of freeing the Jews from Roman rule, one man seems to have tried to manipulate Jesus into revealing His power and authority in very earthly ways. As he realised that Jesus would not be controlled, and was choosing instead to be tried and convicted, he clearly felt terrible remorse. Confessing his sin to those he had used in his manipulation (the priests), he seems to have chosen the moral route by returning the money he had been given to betray Jesus' whereabouts. Thus far, Judas is making amends.

Peter, on the other hand, repeatedly denied that he knew the Lord. Weeping bitterly, he is noticeable by his absence at the foot of the cross. Nowhere is it mentioned that Peter went back to set the record straight with those to whom he lied.

Superficially, Judas seems to do better than Peter, but something else must be going on that was less visible. One man seemed to outwardly repent but inwardly refused to walk in the opposite spirit. For Judas this would have meant seeking to protect rather than expose, seeking to submit rather than manipulatively control. He would have had to depend on God and return to the fellowship of believers, independent of their response. He would have had to acknowledge his failure, and asked to be allowed to serve them, perhaps offering to protect them as they remained in hiding together. But instead he seems to have remained proudly independent and alone, managing his despair through suicide.

At first Peter showed little outward sign of repentance but nevertheless walked in the opposite spirit. After a couple of days, he turned up, racing the other disciples towards an empty tomb in the hope of resurrection. Evidently, he had returned to his brothers, humbled himself and risked their rejection. He had ceased to deny his relationship with Jesus by ceasing to deny his relationship with them.

As I look at Peter's practical relational repentance, I find myself wondering how many times in my life I have been convicted of sin and yet walked the Judas route. These are the times when I feel plenty of remorse and have even verbally acknowledged my sin and yet I have continued in my independence rather than risk walking in the opposite spirit by behaving differently in relationship.

Now that Jesus and I are together in the mess of my hiding place, I need to acknowledge my sinful 'acting out' of unmet need through my relational style. But also, like Peter, I need to walk actively in the opposite spirit in my relationships. Inevitably as I give up my chosen sources of life, cancelling any debts owed to me, I will feel my deep hunger motivating me to turn to Jesus to feed me where I need it most, bringing the hoped-for change from the inside out.

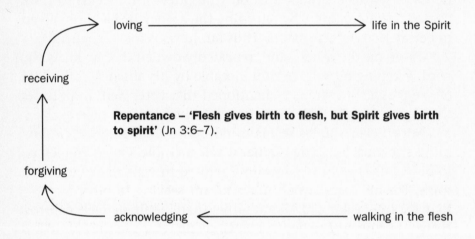

In practice, confessing my sin means being specific about my relational style and the idol I have used to satisfy my crucial parental needs. Because I overcome the enemy by the blood of the Lamb and the word of my testimony, speaking this out aloud to God with another Christian present helps me to face sin, shame and guilt and to receive forgiveness. Their presence offers 'body ministry' as I allow another, on behalf of the Lord, to see my shame and yet accept me in Christ.

I also need to bring any idolatrous relationships (with people or things, sexual or otherwise, fantasy or in the flesh) to Jesus to be rightly severed. In the name of Jesus and having acknowledged it fully, I can put into His body my sin, its effect in my life, my guilt and shame. Jesus stands accused and I am declared innocent. I may also need to renounce in His name all influence and activity of the evil one through this sin and any idolatrous relationships, actively closing any doors in my mind or body that I have opened to the enemy.

Then I need to receive forgiveness, allowing Jesus to pay the debt that I owe. I respond to God as His dependent creature by renouncing my pride (that essentially says that the cross is not enough) and receiving God's mercy in my time of need, however often I need it. In renouncing my fleshly independence and its fruit seen in my relational style, I can invite the Spirit of Jesus to come and dwell in this formerly stony part of my heart and to develop His fruit here.

The first fruits of true repentance undoubtedly involve speaking and practically acting out that repentance to those I have wrongly used and wounded. So I set myself a long-term goal about my ways of relating.

Long-term goal: to give up control in relationship with my daughter, trusting myself and her into the hands of God.

To reach that long-term goal, and as a means of beginning to face and feel my underlying needs, I can set a short-term goal about my ways of relating. Short-term goals need to be specific, measurable, achievable, realistic and time boundaried. SMART goals help me to succeed and therefore gain hope for further challenge and change. If I set an unrealistic and therefore unachievable goal then I am more likely to fail. Like most folk, when I fail I tend to give up and quietly forget about the process of change.

SMART goal: irrespective of how I feel and the dangers she will face, for the remainder of her trip away, I will thoroughly respect her choices to remain or return without requiring her to comply with mine. In practice this means I will not nag her to come home or avoid potentially dangerous situations, but will continue to lay her down prayerfully before God as His child.

This goal is specific (in that it describes a particular way of communicating and relating). It is measurable (she will be able to tell me if I have nagged her or not). It is currently realistically achievable for me (at my level of internal healing, I think I do trust God enough to practise letting her go for the next few months). It is time boundaried by the length of her trip, which encourages me to try because I know that this period will come to a definite end.

Inevitably, as the months go by and I 'walk the talk', I do feel my hunger for safe connection because it is no longer temporarily satisfied by controlling the life of another. In my hunger I am motivated to turn to Jesus as together we clean up my hiding place and explore the historic roots of my sin, clearing the mess at its very foundation. In this I may need to remain accountable to others who can offer me encouragement, challenge, emotional and prayer support while I work it through. Keeping short (even very short) accounts with God and others can be vital.

In the long term, full confession means bringing into the light not only my sin, but also my unresolved emotions, my woundedness and the sins against me. Simply starting on the road of dealing with my independent actions is daunting since the process of engaging with my immense spiritual hunger seems like madness. Depending on how bad it is, I may even feel that I will lose my mind or that I will not survive.

Some of us with entrenched idolatrous issues will need very consistent, compassionate support to turn from wrong sources of life towards the living God. It may also take time as well as support. Some of the 'games' we play both inside and outside relationship are dealt with in an instant. Others have been allowed to grow and develop for so long that they literally take a lifetime to break. That is OK. We are saved. God is more patient with us than we are with one another or ourselves. His grace is sufficient.

One of my most necessary and difficult repentant actions involved saying no to an enmeshed relationship that for a whole year had torn apart my marriage and my soul. I remember a moment, many years ago now, walking away from a car that held the woman in whom I had wrongly invested my entire being. As I continued to walk away, my resolve to maintain that 'no' somehow grew stronger. The objective adult in me felt good about refusing sin. I had realised that what was being offered would never satisfy. I was made for something better and my family certainly deserved much better from me as a wife and mother.

In the days that followed, the raw emptiness at my core surfaced fully and I found a much harder choice before me. I could opt out and drown in hopelessness, or I could choose life. I would like to say that I chose life because I trusted that God would meet me in my need and I wanted to be obedient to Him. Like most of us, my motives were less spiritual. In reality, I chose to stay alive for my children, those who dependently needed me and whose need was entirely appropriate. As I look back, I see that at least I was deferring self-gratification and beginning to think of someone else's needs before my own. It was a step.

I had no idea how I was going to survive emotionally in the turmoil and shame that would inevitably follow as I dealt with the aftermath of renouncing emotional dependency. Turning from my sin had been my first necessary action. But with such stubborn independence at the core of my being and with such overwhelming spiritual hunger, what were the practical steps I needed to take in order to turn towards God as He is, and how could I find life in Him?

CHAPTER 7

THE REALITY OF THE CROSS (II)

Whatever idol I have chosen to use to manage my parental needs, even my physical parents, I need to give that up in whatever way I can, one step at a time. I also need to acknowledge that my current demands and difficulties in both parental and peer relationships are usually rooted in my childhood experience of love:

'When I was a child, I talked like a child, I thought like a child, I reasoned like a child:

No one is up to loving me properly. I must protect myself from further pain.

God isn't fallen. He is holy and good, and is more than able to meet my needs.

'When I became a man, I put childish ways behind me' (1 Cor 13:11).

I have to turn from my idols, leave 'home' and grow up in Christ. I am not a child any more. When I was a child, my independent choices were a little more understandable though still without excuse. Although I attempt to convince myself that I did not know any better then, God says He revealed himself sufficiently to me through creation, yet nevertheless extended me His grace, drawing me towards repentance through His loving kindness. Now as a reasonably well-taught Christian adult, I can begin to trust that everything I need is made available to me through Christ. By recognising and refusing my idolatry, I can get on with being one of God's people rather than remaining a slave to the gods of my warped thinking.

Paul actually uses the word 'abolished' for 'put behind me'. To suddenly abolish my idolatry can be extremely difficult, depending upon the nature of that idol and the magnitude of the foothold or stronghold that I have allowed. For example, it is impossible for people to live without food, so that those of us with eating compulsions have great difficulty in completely freeing ourselves of our dependency, simply because we cannot physically live without that which has been our god. It is also impossible for people to live without relating at one level or another, so that those of us with relational compulsions need to choose extremely carefully with whom we relate and our boundaries in those relationships. But all these things are possible with God.

In practice, my idolatry in relation to my daughter feels quite easy to 'abolish' or put behind me for good. Perhaps less easy to ditch is my idolatry towards women in general. Years ago now, by the grace of God, I largely gave up emotionally dependent relating with women, moving towards them to 'get' security. In all kinds of ways, through His healing, redemptive work in my life, I now experience myself as thoroughly heterosexual. But it has taken a lot longer to slowly forsake my self-protection in relation to women: the ways in which I keep my distance in order to manage my need for security and the inevitable disappointment in female relationships. As I think about socialising with women friends, I feel anxiety from my infancy rising: 'Will I be OK? Will I be safe?' Objectively, all my friends are trustworthy yet still fallen human beings. Dare I put aside my relational style of withdrawal and isolation and relate more consistently with warmth and vulnerability whatever the reception? A useful SMART goal here might be to take a day off work and arrange to meet up socially with another woman who is likely to want to give me her friendship. This may seem simple for you. It has not been so simple for me.

I can choose this so that I learn to love my friends, but also so that I stop trying to minimise my own thirst for unconditional love from women. Rather than manage it, I want to face and feel the pain, disappointment and helplessness of less-than-perfect relationships with women. Here I will face afresh the reality I have been avoiding – that I am a victim of the fall.

Victims of the fall

We are all victims of the fall. In some sense, even God is a 'victim' of the fall. In creating me in His image, He so respected that image that He gave me the power to impact Him negatively, through my mistrust, disrespect and breaking of His boundary. Unlike me, God does not react defensively to His wounds. Instead He feels the pain of them, yet seeks a just reconciliation while remaining thoroughly loving. This is the *message* of the cross. This is the *message* He longs that I communicate to others when I am a victim of the fall.

However, when bad things happen to me I feel helpless and confused and tend to react in ways that reduce my confusion and helplessness. Unconsciously the first thing I do is blame God, the person I believe is meant to be in charge, before I start blaming anyone else. In every human heart, the reality is that God gets a great deal of 'flak' for the painful impact of the fall. Typically I cast Him as the agent of sin, even the author of evil, and so harden my heart a little more against Him. Usually I am more concerned with my woundedness than my sin, and see all suffering as bad for me, which it is not. As C.S. Lewis says, I easily confuse the strong, fierce and ruthlessly other-centred love of God with His kindness, demanding that He relieve my pain now rather than eternally. I do not want to be loved by God as He defines love through the fellowship of sharing in Christ's suffering. I only want God to be nice.

Actually God longs that we respond like Job to the problem of pain. Job remained in a place of helplessness and confusion, crying out to God for a mediator who was able to lay a hand on them both. In other words, Job recognised his need of a living bridge between a human being in agony and a good and holy God who allows suffering. If I responded like Job, I would be more concerned with my sin than my woundedness. I would recognise that because of the fallenness in all our lives, God carefully allows me to suffer within the boundaries He has set, simply because He is ruthlessly other-centred. My suffering and what I make of it will never add anything to God. Nothing can. But there is a possibility that if I trust Him in it, my suffering will add something to me.

Remarkably, pain has the potential to do me good if I allow it to shape me more in the likeness of God as He reveals Himself at the cross. If I really believed this then I would accept that God's love is offered in tension with His kindness. I would fix my eyes on God's permanent pain relief in eternity rather than my self-administered 'aspirin' now. Ultimately, I would prefer to be loved with the only love that God has to offer, rather than have Him be nice. However I respond, the problem of pain wakes me up to the necessity of choice in relation to God: trust or mistrust, dependence or independence. As Lewis says, pain is God's megaphone to rouse a deaf world and surely this is His purpose in allowing it.

So will I be as He is, as faithfully and fully represented in Christ? Will I choose self-denial? Will I respect and love God even though He seems to slay me, even though He seems invisible, absent or non-existent amid evil? Or will I be as the evil one, making self-centred autonomy my god so that my comfort is under my own control? Can I look back on my wounds and, like the apostle Paul, thank God in every circumstance?

What I can do is learn to hate the sin against me rather than the sinners. I can also learn to trust God through each twist and turn in my story as He weaves together His simple goodness with the simple evil of others. As Lewis describes it, the resulting tapestry is God's own complex and wonderful good for my life. More than this, I can learn to thank God that He woos me towards Himself, even though this may include suffering. If I was to believe the reasonable premise that a good God would not allow any unnecessary wounding in the life of His beloved child, then perhaps I would be shocked at the magnitude of the damage and pain that was needed in order for His voice to get through to me and my faith to be vindicated. The question I am then left with is not an angry *'Why have you let this happen?'* but more a humbled and shocked *'Am I so deaf to you, God, that the message has had to be this loud?'*

So pain not only rouses me to the problem of choice in relation to God, but as Job discovered, it also rouses me to the necessity and pursuit of the cross. The crucified body of Jesus is the only place where an agonised human being can meet with God. This is the place where, for both God and humanity, the horror of being a victim of the fall is faced and felt in full. This is the place where we both finally find intimate fellowship in our suffering. When I would rather enjoy the fellowship of sharing in His sufferings than comfort myself independently and alone, then I begin to thank Him. But first I might have to face and feel my anger at Him, at others and finally at the sin against me. And secondly I have to feel the helplessness at my core. I have to face the same confusion as Job and listen to the same questions from God. And this is my journey. This is yours. Like Job, this is our faith on trial before creation. This is our vindication as a son and heir. This is the problem of pain. Am I willing to be a co-heir with Christ, whom God has allowed to be moulded by suffering as well as goodness? Or do I remain satisfied with something less?

Emotional and spiritual pain is therefore my friend rather than my enemy. Like its physical counterpart, it indicates that something is amiss. Probably much like you, I have been taking emotional and spiritual painkillers all my life. Having been so drugged with some means of comfort or other, now I must begin to feel the pain that will motivate me to come to the cross.

Many folk coming into my counselling room have experienced a breakdown in the effectiveness of their idols. The resulting unmet need and agony of soul is what typically motivates them to seek help. They are actually in an enviable position. In His mercy towards them, God has allowed their idol to 'die' so that they are roused out of their deafness to hear the still small voice of the *message*. Perhaps the rest of us do not realise our plight because our idols are providing for us very nicely, thank you very much. You and I may look on folk seeking counselling as if they have a problem and we do not. It could actually be the other way around. At least those in the counselling room recognise their need for sustenance and help.

Perhaps you and I are blind and deaf to the extreme fragility of our situation. Whatever your idol, whatever mine, these created things are actually useless to sustain us simply because they are not really a source or sustainer of life at all. I am not advocating here that we should all be in counselling. But you and I need to wake up to the fact that Jesus has come to call 'sinners' (those who know that something is desperately wrong with the way they live their lives) rather than those 'righteous' in their own sight. According to Jesus, there is something really OK about knowing you need help and something really not OK about thinking you do not. To deny my pain, to shirk my suffering, is to avoid the very cross that God has uniquely allowed for me. It is a cross that He invites me to touch, to grasp and to bear upon my shoulders, that I might follow His Son and fellowship with Him. This cross that is distinctively my own is not simply the persecutions and difficulties that I face today and tomorrow as an adult. It began at my beginning and I ignore its presence in my early years at my own great peril, and certainly risk the peril of others as I refuse to allow those years to be actively redeemed: *'What comes to you quite contrary to your choosing, thinking, desiring, that is where you must follow, there I am calling, there you must be a pupil, there it is the high time, your teacher has come'.*[5]

I begin to grasp my own cross by facing and feeling the problem of my fallen generational and physical inheritance together with the wounds arising from unmet parental and peer needs. As an adult in Christ I can return to these issues, these specific points of origin for my foolish thinking and independent choices for self-centred comfort. In this, I can explore exactly how my boundary may have been trespassed, how my legitimate longing for perfection may have been thwarted and how I feel about that, but without the independent defences this time.

Perhaps I can learn a lesson from God in this. How does He deal with the impact of the trespass of His boundary? He does not broadcast a message of cheap forgiveness: *'It's OK, I'll just forget about what you did to me. Let's sweep it under the carpet and start over again. We'll pretend it didn't happen.'* Nor does He broadcast a message of mass and instantaneous annihilation: *'That's it, you've done it now. You're all dead meat as from yesterday. Be unmade!'* Instead, amazingly, He seeks a completely just redemption, a buying back of relationship. In His righteous wrath, He chooses to remember the trespass in full at the cross, the complete summation of the effect of the fall, in the punishment of His Son. He does this in order to remember it no more, to forgive. For God to forgive a trespass of His boundary means He considers the debt for that trespass paid in full, allowing the relationship to be mutually and respectfully restored as if the trespass had never occurred.

Being made in His image, I am called to communicate this same *message*. I am to use the cross in the same way, remembering in full the impact of any trespasses against me, the inherited woundednesss of my family tree, and the legacy of imperfect biology in order to remember them no more. Denial of my wounds simply maintains my sinful relational strategies. In this God calls me to honestly acknowledge myself (with all my wounds and sinful choices and image-bearing), others (with all their wounds and sinful choices against me and their image-bearing) and most of all Himself (a sovereign God who is good and for me, allowing evil while not being its author).

As an adult in Christ, I need to accept, respect and re-educate the wounded part of me. It even helps to begin to relate to this aspect of myself almost as if she was a different person. In some ways she often is a very split-off part of myself. The adult in Christ is the part that believes and acts as if God is good. The wounded part of me can seem relatively unredeemed in comparison, and it is out of this that I tend to make sinful choices in order to independently supply my parental and peer needs. I need to offer her God's tender compassion by sharing His gospel. Whether she is the adult I was three weeks ago, or the teenager or child I once was, she needs salvation. Her wounds drag her kicking and screaming to the cross as unknowingly she feels His pain. There, as she discovers the deepest possible empathy offered by Jesus, she also needs to find hope for some kind of resurrection this side of heaven.

The adult I am in Christ can foster and nurture this needy part of me until she allows God as the perfect parent (or perfect spouse, the perfect friend, etc.) to adopt her, provide for her and heal her. This is the next stage of the discipleship journey: to take authority in Christ and rule with compassion over my wounded self. Rejecting this part of me, like denial, maintains my sinful relational strategies: *'Let the little children come to me and do not hinder them, for the kingdom of God belongs to such as these. I tell you the truth, anyone who will not receive the kingdom of God like a little child will never enter it'* (Mk 10:14–15).

Acknowledging grief and loss before the cross

I can do self-rejection. In fact, it is probably one of the ways of relating to myself that I have done best over the years. But, interestingly enough, not uniformly over the different stages of my life.

When I counsel some folk, they begin to relate to their wounded self and suddenly connect, feel compassion, nurture and appropriately reprove this part of themselves. It has been a little different for me. For example, when I consider the adolescent I once was, I do have a lot of time for her. She was a confused kid. Her gender identity, her sexuality were all scrambled. She spent most of her time trying to find out whether she was male or female, straight or gay. When she found that teenage relationships left her emptier than before, she sought an alternative strategy. She knuckled down to academic life and became obsessed with work instead. But I like her. I feel compassion towards her. I gently educate her about Jesus. Her wounds are a gift to me, stretching me back two thousand years to tell me about His suffering. There we sit at the foot of the cross as He bears her sin and dies in her place.

As she looks at me I give her hope. Someone must have loved her well for her to have grown into me – a wife, a mother, a friend. She begins to see that there must be a God who has sent and loved her in the same way He has sent and loved His Son, raising Him from death to life. Suddenly she knows the power of the resurrection and my gender-confused teenage heart is being redeemed. Consequently I experience myself as more wholly female and heterosexual than ever before.

But when I turn to the much younger child I once was or the infant adrift from her mother for the first few months of her life, the adult in me has a different reaction. Looking at photos of significant years or life-events can often help us face and feel our hidden emotions. As I explored family photo albums I found myself deeply ashamed of the infant I was, reluctant to show these photos to others. An even more impacting tool can be to choose a soft toy or an object to represent the wounded part of ourselves or maybe even a significant person in our lives. Using a soft baby doll to represent the infant I was, I found that I reacted strongly. I wanted to harm her then ignore her.

I have not liked that infant much. My emotions, choices and underlying thinking have all been negative towards her, as if I am her very critical parent. I have seen her as flawed, not worth providing for, guilty and totally responsible for her mother's emotional and mental problems. After all she would not have been left for so long alone in the nursing home if there were not something wrong with her. However crazy that sounds, that has been my internalised self-perception for many years: *'I'm flawed. I'm bad. I'm the guilty one. I'm responsible for bad things happening.'*

Such beliefs are the foundation and fuel behind self-harming actions in my life. Such beliefs are also normal from the perspective of a traumatised baby in a fallen world: *'as I experience my world, so I am.'* My world was 'bad' and seemingly rejecting towards me, so I concluded I was bad and rejectable.

As life went on, I see that I actually grew up playing the 'critical parent' to myself, living out of my initial perceptions of my nurturing environment. Why did I come to such conclusions? A young child cannot differentiate between the accidental and the deliberate, nor take into account the wider impact of unintentional issues like illness, redundancy or war. Their world is interpreted egocentrically, as a statement about themselves. So when, as a baby, I experienced my mother behaving irrationally and then going away, I perceived those actions as deliberate choices on her part. My mother's post-natal mental problems could not be grasped as separate from me. I did not have the adult capacity to turn around and say: *'It's OK that my mum seems crazy one day and is absent the next. She's actually quite poorly. I do hope she gets better soon. Poor Mum.'*

Likewise, when my father chose to place me in the care of a nursing home and then later reintroduced me to my mother who had previously proved unstable, as an infant I interpreted those choices egocentrically, as a statement about myself. As a baby I did not have the adult capacity to turn around and say: *'It's OK that Dad leaves me in a nursing home and then gives me back to Mum. He has to make the best of a bad job and get back to work to provide for the family. Mum is better now, anyway, after the hospital treatment.'*

'It's also OK that psychiatrists solve the problem through administering treatment to my mum so that she cannot even recall that she had carried or given birth to me. The medical system is trying its best.'

Of course, as a baby I did not have words in my head to form beliefs like these. To access my self-perception at that age, I need to 'speak' in her 'binary' language of body movements (touch or withdrawal), sounds (silence or screaming), emotions (hate or love) and images (bad face or good face).

When I try to 'listen' to what she has been trying to communicate to me all these years, initially I 'hear' the baby silently screaming her agony of soul, hating herself and the world. Then she stills herself into non-feeling, literally turning from relationship body, soul and spirit. There are no images, no face of 'other' in her world, either good or bad. On her own, with no one from whom to draw identity, her world is empty of people other than herself. In an effort to visually communicate something of her worldview, I drip blue paint onto paper. This is a self-image, surrounded by 'blue', bonded with 'blue, completely alone. Within this blue, thoroughly safe 'womb' there is peace. The thought of a human piercing through the canopy to connect with me arouses extreme panic. In this part of my heart, I have absolutely no desire to emerge from this haven of isolation.

To believe that I am loveable and yet find that my huge infantile need for good parental care remains unmet, this is hell (where a potentially loveable person is ultimately separated from a good god). It is much less confusing to conclude that something is profoundly wrong with me, which explains the (apparently) poor treatment I experience.

To overcome such a high level of self-rejection ('I hate me'), I have literally covenanted myself as an adult to the baby I was. Just as Father God covenants Himself to us and therefore promises Himself, His provision and protection, so I have promised my daily loving attention and maternal fostering, aiming to bring that wounded baby into the presence of God through Jesus to be perfectly parented. For me, writing and signing a certificate of foster care has produced a complete turn around in my reactions to myself:

Certificate of Foster-Care

Roselyn Monica Abbott, the adult in Christ, commits to whole-heartedly adopting baby Ros, with all her frailties and broken-

ness. She commits to parenting her appropriately until the baby can trust God (as Father, Son and Holy Spirit) to parent her fully. She agrees to carefully carry this baby, protecting her not exposing her, caring for her unconditionally and not rejecting her.

In return, she requires that as an adult she is given respect by the baby for her adult choices, responsibilities and boundaries. The adult also commits to protecting the baby from any woundedness or self-harm reactions from other childhood stages, to enable the process of integration, so that Roselyn as adult, child and infant may become whole and complete in Christ.

Biblical covenants between God and His people involve terms, conditions and expectations, the presence of witnesses, a tangible sign or symbol of the covenant and even a commitment to selflessly protect the weaker party. There is every reason to copy God's model and offer the same as Christ towards myself.

In the past I have had insufficient hope in God to receive such a promise. First, to build up that necessary hope, I have needed something like God but with 'skin on' to minister appropriate love to the infant in my heart: holding her, looking at her, remaining with her. This is surely one of the purposes of community. Since relationship is the essence of existence, then a biblical philosophy of 'people-helping' must be founded upon the theory that the most important thing each of us has to offer is our real self. I believe that the necessary leap of faith towards transforming repentance is more likely to occur when we begin to be vulnerable in appropriately intimate, well-boundaried relationship 'with skin on'. This is why Jesus came in the flesh and has called us to be 'little Christs' to one another.

The infant in my heart began to hope and believe that there might be a God who is not fallen and who is ultimately good when I had some 'good enough' experiences of His maternal love from others to whom I was relating. The maternal goodness that I receive through spouse, family, friends and colleagues alike is such that finally I now have hope enough to receive and dwell in the goodness of the promised foster-care.

But the cost of such a promise to myself is huge, and involves feeling all kinds of emotions I would rather disown or drown through some painkiller. Once I begin to overcome self-rejection through accepting myself, as I dive down to expose the wounds at my core, I find demandingness and hatred of others: *'You must love me and if you don't, I hate you!'* This is subtly designed to make me independently powerful in my powerlessness. Essentially I conclude that others are not OK. My blaming of others reduces my confusion and powerlessness when I cannot ensure with certainty that others will provide well for me.

Below this I discover the confusion I have been trying to avoid: *'Why don't you love me?'* This in turn overlays my inbuilt helplessness: *'I need you to love me.'* So I find to my horror that dependence has written this eternal, irremovable script that necessitates trust in care-givers who may actually be evil rather than good. Try as I might through independence, I cannot rewrite this script. I need because God has made me needy, and needing requires trust. This is my fundamental problem.

In practice, God invites me to face both my appropriate response and my inappropriate reaction to the trespassing of my boundary. The appropriate response is righteous anger. The inappropriate reaction is contempt (for self and others). But as I do this, my interpretation of the fifth commandment seems to get in the way: *'Honour your father and your mother, as the LORD your God has commanded you, so that you may live long and that it may go well with you in the land the LORD your God is giving you'* (Deut 5:16).

The dictionary tells me that to honour means to have high regard for, to offer special respect, to hold as significant for good. When the Honours List is drawn up in the UK, theoretically we seek to praise certain folk for their positive contribution to our society. As we do this, we are not saying that everything they offered was brilliant. We merely seek to affirm them for the specific good they gave. For example, when we honour past prime ministers, we do it to applaud their commitment to our whole community, to thank them for the long, long hours they served us. The fact that many of us may disagree with their politics and believe that some of their choices may have damaged our economy or culture or national security is neither here nor there. They have attempted to serve. They have given their lives to the nation for a period of time. This is worth applauding. Hopefully, the nation aims to honour what is good and noble, amid awareness of the bad we may see and acknowledge.

In the same way, I honour my parents as I acknowledge and celebrate the ways they looked like God as they provided for me, fulfilling their responsibilities towards me in communicating the *message*. In the ordering of His commandments, God invites me to pay particular regard to these special relationships, above all other human relationships (including spouse and children) because the child-parent relationship is by nature dependent. My relationship with my parents is a kind of ongoing practical workshop for my relationship with God.

As I honour my parents who are seen, I will more easily honour God who is unseen. Another of God's discipleship lessons here. I start with what is in front of my nose before I go on to the hard stuff. In acknowledging and celebrating their specific communication of the *message*, I honour God's workmanship in my parents and so I honour God as the *message-maker*. As I receive that *message* more fully, I begin to become more truly myself, the one that the true person in them actually always hoped that I would be.

As we have seen, there are the two equal and opposite errors that I might typically fall into with any relationships. Either I blame others and can see no good in them (here my anger, confusion and pain are in the way). Or else I hold them up as paragons of virtue, sweeping their failures under the carpet without actually seeking to honour people in a godly way that does not excuse them. By doing the latter I am actually honouring evil as well as good. I am not straining my ears to hear the *message*, but instead taking on board all the 'white noise' of the fall:

> *A full acknowledgement of human responsibility and therefore guilt, far from diminishing the dignity of human beings, actually enhances it. It presupposes that men and women, unlike the animals are morally responsible beings, who know what they are, what they could and should be, and does not make excuses for their poor performance.[6]*

In the same way that God honours me by respecting the image of His sovereignty within me, He calls me to honour everyone else. I cannot truly celebrate the unique good that God offers through others unless I know what it is specifically, and to do that I must separate it from what is not so good. I need to fully acknowledge the role and responsibility of others in relation to me, owning both the positives and the negatives. This is a difficult task since like everyone else I would rather have the fairy tale of unconditionally loving parents, siblings, teachers, pastors, friends, partner and even children.

As I focus on my specific wounds that are hidden behind the mask of my relational style, I need to be willing to temporarily set aside adult rational objectivity and work with my possibly very irrational, subjective perceptions. It is not life as it actually was that unhelpfully affects me now, but life as I saw it when I was hurt. It is this internal reality, this perception that generates my problematic relational style. For example, it really matters very little to a needy child if a parent or a family or a social system has all the rational excuses in the world, if a parental need remains unmet for any reason, the ensuing pain is life-threatening. Each heart really does know only its own pain. So it is only as I am willing to work with what I unconsciously perceive that I will later find real objectivity in Christ.

So as I come, in my brokenness, before the crucified body of Jesus, I can choose to feel the heavy weight of being a victim of the fall. As I specifically name any conscious or unconscious sins against me, the wounds of imperfect biology and generational weaknesses, I come face to face with the damage I have experienced in terms of unmet parental and peer needs. Listing my losses both then and subsequently, I begin to painfully acknowledge 'what might have been'. And so I begin to grieve.

As my discomfort emerges that I have sought so long to avoid, I must face, feel and rightly express into Jesus any anger I feel about being a victim of the fall without causing more pain and trauma to others or myself. Beneath the anger of my grief are pain, disappointment and confusion. Rather than continue to deny these emotions or blame them on others, I need to learn godly suppression, holding onto strong feelings triggered by everyday circumstances, expressing them into the wounds of Jesus.

Coming to terms with my loss in these ways allows my emotions to be expressed controllably and in safety. This is not a 'once and for all' deal. It takes time and effort of will to allow my anger, sadness, pain, fear and disappointment to leak away into the cross. As I do this, I begin to allow Jesus to take my place as a victim of the fall so that my wounds becomes His, and in exchange His comfort becomes mine. I literally begin to agree with what He has already achieved. Standing between myself and those who have sinned against me, either generationally or directly, His back takes the beating of the sin I believe I have suffered. Standing between myself and the frailty of my biology, His body takes the physical wounds and disability I have experienced. He becomes the victim of the fall on my behalf. His face turned towards me radiates compassion and love:

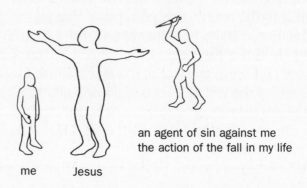

an agent of sin against me
the action of the fall in my life

me   Jesus

When I look at Jesus this way, I begin to see Him as bigger than any possible sin against me, bigger than any disability or wound I seemed to sustain. Now I can gain some objectivity, releasing these things and their painful impact into the body of Jesus, leaving them there. They are rightfully His, not mine. He claimed them two thousand years ago.

What does this process look like in practice? For example, what has it been like for me to feel the pain of infant trauma? Indeed, how can I feel such pain when I do not even remember the events? The Holy Spirit will lead me into any truth about my story that is good for me to know. The fact that I do not consciously remember being a baby does not hold back His work. As I have sought wisdom from Him about the roots of my problematic relational style with women, God has revealed something of my perceptions of the first few weeks of my life. Even if my current understanding is inaccurate, it is nevertheless my unconsciously held perception, and this is the actual basis of my current emotional and behavioural reactions. I need to hold this perception lightly on my hand before Him, acknowledging that a needy infant sees things very differently from an adult. Indeed, for any work with any of my memory, I need to acknowledge that what I perceive is unlikely to be the absolute truth of events. I also find myself susceptible to the suggestions of others about what 'might have happened'. At every point, I need to realistically weigh up before God and others any apparently recovered memory, pleading with God to keep me always from vain imagining. In the end, all I can and must deal with is my perception. In my experience, as long as I keep it and own it as only my enfeebled, fallen worldview rather than objective fact, I reduce the risk of inappropriately blaming others.

My gracious and compassionate God will often answer my prayers in these areas by providing an 'action replay' workshop in the here and now. Circumstances will squeeze me into facing and feeling something of a past event. God is giving me an opportunity to process it properly this time at the cross and thereby relate more receptively with Him. He is extremely patient with me as I visit these 'workshops', learning my life-lessons step by step. Sometimes I may have to repeat the workshop many times before the penny drops.

Writing this book has been one of God's workshops. Several weeks of isolation has reminded my body, my soul and my spirit of those weeks I spent in the nursing home as a baby. I sit alone at the computer day by day. Interruptions are met with irritation and at times strong anger. Sometimes I suppress my anger rightly, putting it on hold in the hands of God until I can discover with Him what it is about. Sometimes I express the anger wrongly: friends or family get it in the neck because they disturb my peace.

What words are beneath my anger? I want to be alone, drifting into non-being... Go away world! *Go away, Daddy! Why must he come to visit me and disturb this safe isolation? Don't put us* (Mum and me) *back together on any account! I hate us. I hate everyone!'* As an adult, I experience depression, unmotivated to be involved in anything outside the task of writing, absorbed in my own thoughts. My only wish is to be under the 'blue' and typing. The infant is angry with her father for putting her in the nursing home to begin with and for then intermittently reawakening her relational senses as he visits from time to time. She believes she has been abandoned by care-givers. Having defended herself against abandonment, she is then regularly reminded of her colossal need for loving relationship by her father's visits, like a torture technique that leaves her to starve then shows her food every now and again without ever actually feeding her.

As I begin to grasp what God is doing here, I connect with the baby through my thinking and journalling. Long ago she mostly felt and processed the pain and confusion of separating badly from her mother. Now she is left with her defence of silence and relational withdrawal. Very still in the arms of Jesus who is with her whether or not she perceives Him, her eyes are closed and her frame is tightly rigid. Physical touch elicits pain. Alone she is a safe and self-contained island.

Because the baby is still 'remembered' in the body of the adult I am, I allow myself to be held by prayerful friends. After prolonged hesitation I curl up under loving touch as I finally dare to trust. Pain seeps into hands modelling Jesus and my harsh but oddly quiet scream of agony emerges. Huge waves of sadness sweep over me and a longing that has lain dormant for over forty years revives. A longing for love.

I find myself easily rationalising my father's choices. In such a position, it is as if I say to the baby: *'Your feelings do not matter. He did what he had to do at the time.'* Temporarily, I need to set aside those rationalisations and find a way of expressing my deeper feelings. Under the guidance of the Holy Spirit, if I were able to express something directly to my father as I saw him then, perhaps something could be resolved. Perhaps God will give me insight and enable me to forgive. I place an empty chair next to me and imagine sitting opposite my father. But actually it is not my father as he is that I need to speak to, it is the man as the baby saw him. Also, it is not just me that needs to speak but both the adult I am today and the baby as she saw herself then. As I do this, I am neither seeking to communicate with the dead nor requiring that my perception is the absolute truth. In the presence of God, I need to feel and express the emotions that arise from that early perception of events. So I begin to speak from my chair: *'Why is work more important than me* [confusion]*? Why don't you love me?'*

In order to discover how I see my father, I take his place in his chair. I reply: *'I'm tired, stressed and desperately worried about how things will turn out. I've grasped at what seems like the most obvious solution to the circumstances. I've put you in a home so that you can be cared for. It's clean and clinical. You're safe there. Safe out of harm's way. Now I've got to get back to work. I've got to go. They're expecting me at the office.'*

Returning to my own seat, I retort in anger: *'I'm here! This is my life you are talking about. Can you see me? Wake up and see me! I hate your stupid work. I need you. I need a mum. I need to be loved. Please, please, please love me* [helplessness]. *Be my mummy as well as my daddy. Stop discounting me because I'm little. Will you just open your eyes and see that I'm a person who needs to be loved, not some other problem that has to be neatly sorted out!'*

As I type, my fingertips are hitting the keyboard with vehemence. In the quiet of my office and in the presence of God, my anger emerges rightly this time so that no one is getting hurt. My internalised relationship with my father is becoming more real. I think about what I would say to my mother in the same way, using chair work. Searing pain emerges. There is so much loss on both sides, I can hardly bear to feel it. I see that the issue is less resolved than I thought and there is more that God wants to do here. So I sit as an adult opposite the empty chair where she sits. Beneath the chaos of mental illness, my mother was a warmly relational woman of God. I long to have really known her, to have met her real self just once. Tears begin to communicate my heart better than words.

CHAPTER 8
LEAVING AND CLEAVING FOR REAL

Because I have never before allowed myself to properly grieve that unmet need for safe parental connection, I have spent years detaching from people, requiring them to come through for me perfectly or else suffer my refusal to relate to them. In particular, in my effort to be their judge, jury and jailor, I have bound myself spiritually to my parents as my source of life and through my relational style with them I have exacted the punishment I foolishly believed they deserved. More than this, through the same relational style with others, I have exacted an identical punishment on everyone else who remotely reminded me of them. My sinful reaction seems greater than the initial wound.

Leaving 'home' rightly – releasing forgiveness

'For if you forgive men when they sin against you, your heavenly Father will also forgive you. But if you do not forgive men their sins, your Father will not forgive your sins' (Mt 6:14–15).

When I read this I find myself asking the question: *'Are my sins forgiven through faith in Jesus Christ or not?'* If there are people to whom I have not offered the same full and free forgiveness as God has offered to me, what does that indicate about my standing before God? Do I fear the word of God sufficiently that I will hasten with all possible speed to release from their debts those who I believe may owe me?

Take a typical example. My friend and I have just forgiven one another. Fundamentally we were sinning against God as we related badly. She was unconsciously demanding that I meet her parental need for security. I reacted to her demand with both righteous and demanding anger, requiring her in turn to meet my parental need to be respected. We had each related as a demanding child to a parent, rather than as two adults relating as peers.

Why had we done this? Unconsciously, my friend 'saw' me through the veil of her childhood perception of her mother.

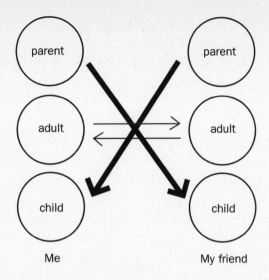

Me | My friend

Because she judged her mum as owing her a debt of security, she acted out that judgement with me. Her self-centred relational style indicated the unforgiveness in her heart towards her mother and towards myself as a woman close to her.

What about me? My superficial hurt was legitimate, but a deeper reaction emerged. The interaction had reminded me of my relationship with my father and so unconsciously, I 'saw' her through my childhood perception of him. Because I judged my

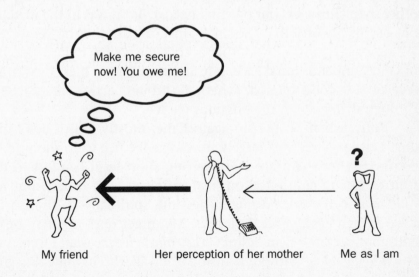

My friend | Her perception of her mother | Me as I am

dad as owing me a debt of significance, I acted out that judgement with my friend. She would have to pay instead of him. My self-centred relational style indicated the bitterness in my heart, both towards my dad and towards others close to me.

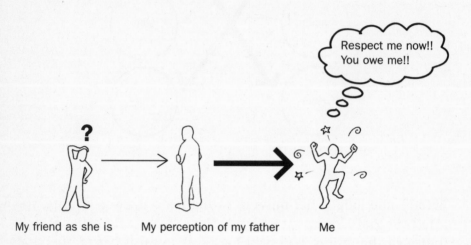

My friend as she is   My perception of my father   Me

Seeing that our reactions were out of order yet our hurts valid, we put those childhood hurts on hold before God and began to discuss the problem. We recognised our faults, said our 'sorrys' and forgave from the heart. The root of the problem was our idolatry and sin against God (demanding that someone or something else other than Him meet our parental needs). But it was in the working out of this idolatry that the sin against one another had emerged. We trespass against one another every time we fail to be a channel of God's unconditional love, refusing to selflessly bless or warmly receive the good offered, whether through action or inaction, through deliberate or unconscious choice.

Sadly, when people sin against me, mostly I stuff down my anger and leave things largely unresolved. I flee from the pain of conflict rather than face it, preferring short-term comfort to the fruit of loving confrontation: real intimacy with others. But my hidden and unresolved anger 'ties' me spiritually to those who have sinned against me. It festers. My anger does not stay righteous, but becomes demanding: *They must give me what I want, and give it to me now!* Without realising it, I walk through life dragging around a list of spiritual soul-ties formed through this bitter idolatry. As the years go by, I become accustomed to their weight and stupidly imagine I have cleared the debts against me. With all this extra burden dragging behind me, is it any wonder I find it so difficult to fully and freely love?

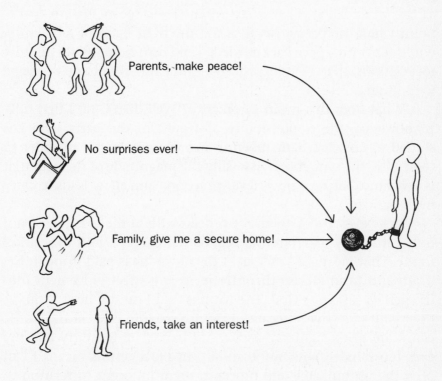

In order for me to 'cleave' dependently to God and interdependently with others, I have to 'leave' my idols behind once and for all. Putting it simply, I need to turn from the 'gods of my fathers' by ceasing to demand from and judge those I believe have wounded me and allow the debts they owe me to be paid in full by Christ. I also need to turn from requiring that my biological inheritance and physical experience be perfect and allow the debt owed through fallen circumstances to be paid in full by Christ.

Forgiveness is simply the first part of repentance. It is the turning from things or people I have used to meet my needs. As I forgive, I begin to repent and so my own sins are forgiven. It is just the way the thing works.

How am I to forgive? My best guess is that it needs to be in the same way that God has forgiven me. While I was still powerless and steeped in sin, God did His part to make the way open for me to return to Him if I chose: *'Father forgive them, for they do not know what they are doing'* (Lk 23:34).

God did not wait until I had realised my error and said sorry to then consider whether or not He would do His part. Remarkably, as the wounded party He has initiated the reconciliation to the point where He patiently offers me the right hand of fellowship, while at my own pace I acknowledge and turn from my sin in order for relationship to be fully restored. And I am asked to do the same with others.

What does this mean in practice? Well, like God, I first fully acknowledge the responsibility and guilt of the party who has sinned against me, remembering my wounds in full in order to remember them no more. Assessing the magnitude of the debt that is owed me, I express my grievance to God and allow Jesus to carry my wounds.

Since everything about me is dealt with at the cross, Jesus not only carries my pain but also bears other people's guilt in relation to me. That means that the debt they owe me is paid through His death and I can release them from my imperfect judgement into the perfect justice of God. The truth is that I cannot hope to judge their guilt objectively because I cannot see into their heart like He can. I am not a righteous judge. My hands are too dirty and my eyes too blinded with my own sin. In practice this means I can offer the unthinkable and proclaim them innocent in relation to me, remembering their sin no more. So I too can patiently offer the right hand of fellowship, while at their own pace they acknowledge and turn from their sin in order for relationship to be fully restored.

Just as God deals with me so I must deal with others, longing for restoration, praying and hoping without demanding, all the time selflessly and boldly loving them with both grace and truth. All that remains for them to do is to repent.

Releasing deep forgiveness in this way comes in stages and God is patient with me in this process. This is just as well since it can take time to forgive deeply from the heart as the Old Testament story of Joseph highlights. Imagine the scene. The older brothers of a teenager have plotted to kill him. Then they think better of it, and instead handle him roughly and sell him into slavery. Years later, despite trials of wrong accusation and imprisonment, the boy has become a man of authority and literally holds the lives of his brothers in his hands.

Has he ever bothered to send regular messages back home or even returned in person to rejoin his family? No.

Once he recognises his brothers for the first time, does he rush into their arms and rejoice at their renewed fellowship? No.

Does he even treat them fairly as he would anyone else in need? No.

Instead Joseph seems to play a game, like a cat with a mouse, wondering whether or not to accuse them falsely rather than face the reality of their ancient crime against him. He seems uncertain about whether he wants to love them or condemn them. The game he is playing has a huge pay off: the power of judgement. But, at the same time, it triggers his grief at their previous actions against him and his deep longing for his father. The agony of the wound that they inflicted so many years ago erupts in a huge catharsis. As he finally feels that wound, Joseph chooses no longer to hold them responsible. It is God's larger plan. They intended it for evil, but God intended it for good. Having faced the agony in full, finally he is able to forgive and re-enter relationship with them, remembering the sin no more. His behaviour towards them communicates mercy in ways that cannot be ignored. But it has taken many years and a great deal of God's refining of that original arrogance (so typical of a seventeen-year-old boy favoured by his father) to enable Joseph to reach this point.

Why does it take so long to forgive? Partly it is because I forget the biblical cycle of cancelling debts every seven years. If I always kept the example of God's mercy towards me in Christ at the front of my mind, I would probably forgive much more rapidly. But I do forget and take God's mercy for granted. Often I need that regular seven-year reminder to review my relationships (e.g. family, work, church), checking out that all my debts and all their debts are cancelled before God. Although this is a protracted length of time, at least every seven years is better than nothing!

Why do I so readily put myself in the place of God and act as judge and jury towards others? If you were to imagine a chain of unforgiveness from me to you forming a soul-tie between us, there are logical but wrong reasons that I put that in place. First, judging you gives me power, where your sin against me had placed me in a position of powerlessness. Secondly, I judge you to maintain hope. If I demand redress, even unconsciously, you may actually change your mind and give me what I want. Sometimes manipulation does work! Lastly, my unforgiveness and judgement is a way of maintaining relationship with you. For example, if you are a British national fiddling your tax returns, you have not loved me or other British nationals well. But I do not have much problem forgiving you because I do not consider our relationship so very critical to my existence. But, if you are a family member who has abused or neglected me, our relationship is sufficiently important to raise my expectations extremely high. If I cannot love you, I will unconsciously judge you and hate you instead rather than lose the relationship all together.

Going to court

'And what does the LORD require of you? To act justly and to love mercy and to walk humbly with your God' (Mic 6:8).

What does it mean for me to act justly? It means that, like God, I should not be afraid to call sin 'sin' and express my grievance at the actions or inactions against me. I need to 'take to court' those who have sinned against me, using God's justice, not my own. God's courtroom is at the cross, this is where His justice rules and is enacted.

Expressing the grievance

Imagine the scene. In God's courtroom, as the adult in me 'holds' the baby I was, who would I put in the dock? Having worked through some of these early issues to do with my mother, the impact upon me of my father's choices stares me starkly in the face. I see that in taking guilt off my mother. I may have put most of it onto my father rather than Jesus.

I set up the courtroom in my mind. In the past I would have put myself in the dock rather than my father, and would have acted as judge and jury against myself. Having recognised that this is simply another way of independently managing my confusion and pain, I stop doing this, and instead I stand in the courtroom as the accuser with my dad as the accused in the dock.

Now, what is the grievance I need to express? My indictment is double-edged. Somewhere in him, at that time, I believe my father instinctively knew that my place as a small infant was with my parents. In spite of this I see that he chose to believe that 1950s British psychiatric culture knew best. Here, short-term separation from parents was not seen as problematic to either party. Also from the baby's perspective, no one seemed to care that after unpredictable behaviour from my mother and the apparent emotional neglect of a clinical environment, I was being returned to a woman whose future behaviour was an entirely unknown.

I need to express this in full before the judge (hopefully this is God but I had better check this out) and jury (objective witnesses alongside me in the here and now), and in particular before the accused (my internalised perception of my father at that time).

Revoking revenge

sinner

By now, I am becoming aware of how, for many years, I have actually judged the accused out of court. I need to assess how much of my previously hidden anger is about inappropriate demand (hating and judging the sinner) or unmet desire for good relationship (hating the sin). I discover that essentially the baby hates her father for being unwilling to 'mother' her.

But I am called to communicate the *message*, to reflect God in every way. In the cross, He has revoked revenge in relation to me.

His judgement is balanced by His mercy and grace. The first step He has taken in this process is to separate out my sin against Him from me as a person. He has judged the sin as not OK and punished it. He is also willing to offer me mercy and grace if I choose to repent. So I need to be like God.

As I stand in the courtroom before the accused, I begin to see that sometimes the sin against me looms large in the foreground, dwarfing my father behind it. At other times, I find that the sin looks puny compared to his brokenness, so that I too easily absolve him of responsibility because he 'had a bad childhood'. As I begin to separate out the sin from the sinner, I aim to allow God to give me His perspective on both. What do they look like?

I see his sin as his choice to believe professionals and obey cultural norms rather than follow his own instincts, because it was convenient for him in terms of his work and personal significance. I also see his sin as his choice to return me unsupervised to my mother rather than monitor the process himself. Fundamentally his needs came before mine.

Having separated that out, I now see the sinner as a man driven by fear of the poverty he had witnessed as a boy; a man determined to provide for himself and his family and therefore keep 'the wolf from the door'; a man who had learnt that achievement and success at work kept you alive; a man who had learnt that to be a man he needed to earn money to care, rather than care directly.

Hating the sin

What do I feel towards the sin? What do I want to do with it? It is OK to hate sin and to focus that hatred at the cross where righteous revenge has already occurred. God hates sin. I need to communicate His *message*. As a Christian, I sometimes foolishly believe that I must not be angry or hate. In reality God is full of anger and hatred, and Scripture overflows with it. I am called to hate what He hates, and what He hates is independence from Him. How am I to express this hatred? Like God, into the body of His Son. In all that the cross was designed to accomplish, His anger is spent. Likewise, for me, there is a time to stop hating, to let go of the anger.

Actually I do hate the sins against me, and at the same time find myself tired of carrying them and their effects in my life. Finally I am becoming willing to let Jesus suffer them instead. In particular, I look afresh at Jesus and see Him being separated from His Father and given into the hands of fallen men who would potentially treat him very badly indeed. I see that I am not alone in my suffering or in my hatred of that sin.

Loving the sinner

Looking at the guilty sinner in the dock, what do I feel? How do I want to relate with him? How do I see someone and their sin against me when I look at them through the crucified body of Jesus? It is not OK to hate people and to continue to reject them in anger. The *message* is fundamentally about compassion, grace, slowness to anger, abounding love and faithfulness. This is the nature of the Lord, maintaining love to thousands, forgiving wickedness, rebellion and sin. Yet He does not leave the guilty unpunished.

My father has unintentionally wounded me, not knowing what he was doing. I now need to accept him in his real identity: bearing dignity, yet wounded, vulnerable and making poor choices out of his own unmet need. I can feel the stirrings of compassion towards him in my heart. I can feel the longing to have known the real person my dad was with godly qualities hidden behind his sin against me. Only God knows his heart and mine. Only he can judge between us. In my own sinful independence, have I any right to condemn him? Indeed, as I have persistently judged him, the consequence is that I have played at being 'God' in his life, standing between him and the only true source of conviction, justice, mercy and grace. God has longed to draw my father towards repentance through His loving kindness. All I have offered is condemnation, blocking God's *message* through me.

So how do I feel now towards my father as the sinner? He seems small and weak against the forces of evil. He looks traumatised. Peering into history, I see the depression that followed the Great War during which my father was born. Fear of poverty hung over Tyneside culture as a curse. I feel compassion for him as a little boy, watching other children starve and seeing grown men subjected to futility. With this perspective, and as an act of the will, I can easily hand my father over to God as the only righteous judge. As I look at God through the cross, what does this judge look like? He seems fair, He seems loving, and He seems like a better and more capable judge than me.

Cutting the ties

Ceasing to judge someone will not only change them, it will also change me. Dealing with my judgemental reactions and the sin against me is essentially focusing upon the spiritual ways in which both I and the sinner have been 'tied' together in co-dependent relationship, each using the other as an idol. Ceasing to judge will set me free spiritually to receive God as He is. But there may be 'ties' in other areas of my functioning which may need to be severed. As I look at the sinner and myself, what kinds of ties remain? What are the remaining cords that bind us together? It is important that every area of functioning is systematically freed through prayer, renouncing the influence of the real enemy, the devil.

Spiritually there may be a tie through the influence of the evil one, particularly if a family curse is involved (such as poverty in this case) or if the sin has involved abuse, or if there are associated generational issues.

Rationally there may be images and thought patterns which have taken root within my thinking through the sin against me, or vows that have been taken unconsciously or consciously.

My will may have been surrendered to the other person in some ways, as I experienced powerlessness in relationship with them. Alternatively, my will may have been allowed to be unboundaried. One of the effects of my father's sins against me is that at a deep level I have experienced myself as powerless (without choice) to ask for the care I require or desire. I have foolishly believed that I have to put up with what I get. I am tired of my compliance and am seeking to invite God to bring His healing into the bruising of my will at such a very young age.

Emotionally, as well as my own emotional reactions to the sin against me, there may have been an inappropriate emotional connection between the sinner and myself, e.g. anger being 'put' into me, or emotional reactions being deadened.

Physically there may be bodily reactions to the sin against me that need to surface and be healed, so that I am physically cut free from the effects of the sin against me, blessing those parts that have been traumatised or neglected. Taking the sword of the Spirit and with the power of the shed blood of Jesus, I can sever the inappropriate ties entirely. If Jesus sets me free, I am free indeed.

Forgiveness and blessing

In return for the curse of the sin against me, can I stand in the courtroom and verbally release forgiveness: *'Father, forgive him, for he did not know what he was doing'*? Forgiveness means agreeing with God by taking the guilt off the accused and putting it onto Jesus. He has died so that everything that bars me from perfection, both sin and spoiling, is destroyed. What does that guilt look like? How does it feel to let Jesus take it for the accused and for me to declare him innocent in relation to me?

Divine forgiveness means more than pardon. The pardoned criminal is still a guilty person. Everybody knows that he committed the sin for which he received his pardon. It is the punishment, not the guilt that is gone. But Christ's forgiveness also means that the sin is gone. The sinner has been cleansed as well as pardoned.[7]

In allowing the guilt to be displaced from my father to Jesus, the latter wears the labels 'abandoner' and 'guilty' rather than my father – who now wears the label 'innocent'. Rather than only ceasing to judge, I am also ceasing to hold another guilty for what I perceive as his sins against me. Any actual guilt on my father's part is now an issue between God and him, rather than with me in the middle. Suddenly the cross seems enormous to me. The baby in my heart is stilled as she gazes at her father. He is her daddy after all, with much to offer that she has never really received before. She begins to hear the sweet strains of the *message* coming through his actions towards her, actions that had always been there but were never before 'heard' untainted by his sin. By the grace of God, I am beginning to enjoy the fruit of acting justly, loving mercy and walking humbly with my God.

Within that courtroom, can I move on another step and even bless my father? Now that he has been dead for a few years what does it mean in practice to bless him or his memory? Perhaps I can start by thanking God for my dad. Maybe I can begin to cherish and enjoy the godly ways in which I and my children are like him. More generally, what God counts a blessing may not immediately be likeable. For example, to lovingly challenge someone to the point of enabling a conviction of their sin against you is a way of blessing them, but they may not immediately enjoy it!

Relating again

As I leave the courtroom in my mind, I have given over the accused to the judgement of God. I am left with what remains of the relationship in the here and now. God has called me to develop an attitude of mercy and grace, remembering the sins against me no more. In this sense, I am called to 'turn the other cheek' and begin to honour my father. Practically speaking, if my dad were still alive, could I begin to pray with heartfelt compassion for him? This would be a first step towards relating afresh.

Like Jesus, I am called to be full of both grace and truth. Jesus came as a gracious gift from the Father and dwelt among us, loving us with His whole heart while we were still sinners. Despite the stench of our sin in His nostrils day by day, despite our many selfish actions against Him, He remained. Even more remarkable, the third person of the Trinity, the unsung hero, remains still. For a moment, can I imagine what it is like to be the Holy Spirit? Century after century, He dwells among us, grieved by our sin, yet persistently leading us into all the truth. This is grace.

In the same way, I am called into righteous relationship even with the one who has sinned against me. Can I look for God's opportunities here? Can I imagine moving towards them with bold, Christ-like love? Can I seek their best interests in God? Am I able to lovingly challenge them when necessary, desiring responsible change in their behaviour towards me?

What if the sinner seems unrepentant and continues to behave in sinful ways towards me? How do I appropriately re-enter relationship? I need to remember that human relationship is designed to communicate trinitarian relationship. I am called to respect the image of God, whether in myself or my neighbour. This means that our boundaries need to encourage that mutual respect. Even Jesus chose where or when He would allow Himself to be sinned against. In not allowing Himself to be harmed before God's time, He put careful boundaries in place. Like Jesus, I am not a doormat. I am an awesome representation of the living God. I need to respect myself as well as others.

The awakening to receive

Where I have hardened my heart in that relationship and subsequently refused to receive any good that the other may have offered me, I now need to allow a softening to occur, knowing that Christ can and does meet me lovingly even through the other person who has wounded me in the past and may, indeed, wound me again. This is bold love. This is the *message*. In this way I awake to the awful truth that it is not my father's sins against me that have blighted my life, but my own sinful reaction. This is the principal focus of Scripture: not that I have been sinned against, but that I have sinned. One or two sins against me, and my typical reaction is to judge and discount all the good that the offending person may subsequently offer. As I did this to my father, I failed to honour him as I should and I also refused the sustenance he aimed to give. Probably much like you, I find I have raised myself on a starvation diet, not necessarily because there was so little provided but because, out of judgement of his errors, I subsequently refused to receive much of what my father offered as a legitimate source of parental love.

To my horror, my conclusion is that I have shot myself in the foot. This realisation has produced a painful awakening to the hardness of my supposedly receptive heart: hardened to parents, family and wider systems sometimes trying to offer their best amid the impact of their own generational garbage; hardened to a faceless world that seems to hand out physical or mental or sexual disability like a rigged game of poker; hardened to God who, all the while, promises to sustain me and whispers the *message* in His still small voice.

CHAPTER 9
REAL FOOD – REAL DRINK

The spiritual nourishment that God sought to offer me through my parents and every other, wider relational system has been tainted by self-centredness. As a result, mostly I have refused to be sustained that way. Tired of the 'fast food' I manipulate from others, I hunger and thirst for my parental and peer needs to be properly met and find myself desperate for real food and real drink that will fill me at my core.

But like Adam, instead of trusting in and drawing upon the unseen God, I want my spiritual sustenance to be tangible – something like God with skin on, something I can see. To answer this problem, amazingly the image of the invisible God has come in the flesh. But that was two thousand years ago. Since then, in a lesser way, Jesus keeps on putting on flesh as you and I allow Him to dwell within us, the physical temple of His body the Church. I cannot moan that I need Jesus now not two thousand years ago. He is here, in you. He looks at me through your eyes. He is here, in me. His hand holds yours through mine. So God the Father has given me a bridge that I can touch and see in order to access His provision. And because He knows that you and I will let Him down, not reflecting His glory, not communicating His *message*, He has even given us something else. Unlike you and me, a simple meal of dependable bread and reliable wine cannot rebel against Him. By His grace it can offer His sustenance in a way that I can feel, taste, smell and even absorb into my belly. You cannot get more tangible or reliable than that.

The theology of the Lord's Supper

How does He do this? First in the upper room as Jesus washes the disciples' feet, you and I are specifically encouraged in our mutual priestly ministry. This is how we are to prepare for His covenant meal, renewing our relationship with God and with one another. Secondly, Jesus gives us the bread and wine, blessed and set aside for the purpose, taken in community together, to use as symbols and sacraments of the real food and real drink that He offers. Through faith, as I bring to the Lord's Supper my spiritual hunger and thirst, created by the sin of others against me and my own sinful independence, He allows the power of His death and resurrection to pour into my life where I need it most.

In all kinds of ways that bypass my rational thinking, through what I touch, see, smell, taste and see, the symbolism of the meal feeds me with wholesome truth about God's unconditional promise to me. I am reminded to trust alone in the death of the Lord Jesus Christ, which 'cuts' the New Covenant. Like an innocent animal sacrificed in an ancient treaty between a king and his vassal, Christ experiences and absorbs the separation and enmity between God and His people, while we receive reconciliation and peace. So when I take this meal in an attitude of faith, I enact my part as a recipient of the treaty. The practical nourishment of bread and wine depict the benefits I gain: spiritual sustenance and resurrection life. As you and I eat and drink together, we express our oneness in community: He is our God and we are His people.

Is there more to it than this? Is this covenant meal designed to simply but powerfully remind me of truth, like a monthly or weekly jog to my memory? Actually, the Lord's Supper is not just a symbol but also a sacrament, a means of imparting spiritual reality into me if I am willing to receive it through faith. Sadly, where we emphasise the symbol rather than the sacrament, we tend to ignore its healing and restorative power. But God has chosen the Lord's Supper as one way of imparting the actual power of the cross into my life within the family setting of the Church. For you and me it is His most reliable and consistent *message*, and the grace He offers at my point of need does change my heart little by little, depending on my willingness to receive.

As a believing participant, sacramentally the Lord's Supper directly provides me with the unconditional love of God through Jesus His Son. I have a secure place in His heart, all the provision I need and a purpose in His kingdom. All the benefits of the New Covenant are mine, not through any merit but as an undeserved gift. In the 'now' of communion, I taste eternal life: an intimate knowledge of God. With the fullness of this blessing still to come, I gain a greater ability to keep the requirement of His covenant: dependence upon Him and love for my neighbour. So as I take the bread and wine, I can offer back my trust in Him and my commitment to be His *message*. Through the faith that He imparts, something real is happening. Something has changed.

Although the treaty of the New Covenant is one way (proclaimed and established by God alone), it is mutually accomplished through the grace of God and the sanctification and perseverance of the saints. Each time I exercise my faith as I take the Lord's Supper, the treaty is both renewed and legally ratified in public. This event has spiritual power both positively in my own life and negatively against my own flesh, the world and the devil. It is effective both to heal me and as a weapon of war.

Of course, I may not take the Lord's Supper in every situation, but only when I have previously consciously removed the blocks to fellowship with God or other believers. Then, having forgiven those who have trespassed against me and having put right the trespasses I have made, I bring to God's table the ways I have broken the treaty, and God does the spiritual repair work, as He has promised to do. As the Holy Sprit makes conscious what has been unconscious in terms of my idols and woundedness, it is entirely appropriate and essential to make use of the Lord's Supper for historic issues as well as those currently known.

Stooping to the cross

The ground before the cross is level. No one deserves or needs it more or less than anyone else. Each one of us is ruined by insidious sin. If you and I were to stand together with the elements of bread and wine carefully placed upon the floor between us, we would both have to stoop to reach them. There is a symbolic truth in this. The cross goes deeper than the depth of both my sin and yours. Much, much deeper. The cross also goes deeper than the depth of both my brokenness and yours. Much, much deeper. In my seemingly righteous state, created by sleight of hand through complex defences and a smattering of cultural propriety, I must stoop to reach Jesus at the cross. He bears more than I care to consider.

In my counselling room I have some stones from the Nazi concentration camp Belsen. By the world's standards, these stones are witnesses to seemingly greater sin and deeper wounds than I will ever know. They cry out for the necessity of a saviour, a redeemer, a healer. But even they must stoop to visit the cross. If the Trinity is the source of creation then the cross is the 'sink'. Before it I am tempted to be a Pharisee, wondering how to identify with such a display of guilt and pain. Yet God calls me to stoop and touch the flesh that hangs there. Here I am to deposit my transgressions, and like the tax collector at the back of the temple, beat my breast and plead: *'God have mercy upon me a sinner.'* God clearly commends such accurate and humble self-understanding. However good and virtuous I appear, internally I am against Him and my heart is deceitful and desperately wicked. I need His infinite mercy moment by moment.

But sin is not all there is to me. There are also my rather meagre wounds. This is the other part of my rubbish that must be deposited at the cross. Once again, will I stoop to touch this flesh that has lost all semblance of humanity? Perhaps Jesus will allow me a little licence to extend the analogy of the Pharisee and the tax collector:

Two men went to church to pray, one a pillar of the Christian community and the other the son of generations of parents who had abused their children. The pillar of the community stood up and prayed about himself: 'God, I thank you that I am not like other men – broken and wounded, ravaged by the sins of others against me. I am whole. My upbringing and family background was exemplary, clearly unlike this man here. My thinking is sound, my emotions are under control and I absolutely never get angry at anything.

But the wounded man cried out loudly in anguish to God because of the injury he had suffered and with agony of soul. He fell upon his knees, and could not even look up to heaven, but beat his breast and said, 'God restore my soul, I feel wounded beyond repair.'

I tell you that this man, rather than the other, went home healed and whole before God. For everyone who exalts himself will be humbled, and he who humbles himself will be exalted.

Throughout the numerous examples of Scripture, particularly in the Gospel of Luke, where Jesus meets one broken human being after another, God also clearly commends an accurate and humble understanding of woundedness. However whole and 'together' I appear on the outside, without the real fruit of the Spirit in my life, I am only able to sustain an appearance of relational maturity in the face of the fall through my personal, independent defences. Control of emotions to avoid conflict is not the same as self-control in order to love. In a fallen world, only the grace of God keeps me appearing relatively civilised and seemingly whole. Which of us can say we are unwounded by the impact of the fall? Which of us can say that we do not feel empty and suffer emotional pain? Which of us can say that we have no need of the stripes of Christ?

So God commends me and blesses me for my honesty and humility about both my wounds and my fallen reactions to those wounds. When I admit my poverty, He seeks to make me rich, graciously bestowing upon me the blessings of His covenantal promise:

> *Blessed are we when we know we are spiritually bankrupt – ours is the kingdom of heaven. Blessed are we when we are grieved in our hearts by the loss of all we had hoped for – we shall be comforted. Blessed are we when we acknowledge our neediness before our God – we will inherit the earth. Blessed are we when we feel our spiritual hunger and thirst for right relationship – we will be satisfied with real food and real drink. Blessed are we when we forgive others, declaring them innocent – we will be forgiven and declared innocent. Blessed are we when all our hidden thoughts and choices and feelings are pure – we will see God. Blessed are we when we seek to resolve conflict rather than ignore it or inflame it – we shall be called sons of God. Blessed are we when we are put down and persecuted because we seek to be in right relationship – ours is the kingdom of heaven.*

(Adapted from Mt. 5:3–10)

Boundaries, conflict resolution and intimacy

The death and resurrection of Jesus Christ communicates God's intention for boundaries, conflict resolution and intimacy in relationship. Boundaries are about separateness, drawing a line between where you start and I begin, between what is your responsibility and what is mine. As I think about boundaries in relationship, what was the message I received about this through my family tree and childhood experience? Did the big people in my life (parents, grandparents, older siblings, teachers, etc.) show respect for other people's bodies, feelings, choices, opinions and longings? Or were boundaries ignored or bulldozed? Was a yes heard as 'yes' and a no as 'no'? Could I do no wrong, or alternatively, could I do no right? What was the message that came through?

When I look at the cross, what is the *message* about boundaries? When God requires punishment for my sins against Him and others, He is saying that the boundaries of others matter, and that breaking those boundaries is a trespass against Him. When He requires punishment for the sins against me, He is saying that my boundaries matter. Whether I have been given far too much licence or imprisoned under the control of another, folk have sinned against me. The abuse or neglect of my boundaries is a trespass against Him. The cross beckons me towards respect for both myself and others, but most of all for God.

Conflict resolution is about how I 'go to court' within relationships when, apparently, a trespass of a boundary has occurred. As I think about conflict resolution in relationship, what was the message I received about this through my family tree and childhood experience? Did the big people in my life model conflict resolution well, by acting justly, loving mercy and walking in dependence upon God? Did conflict mean shaming and punishment way out of proportion to the offence? Or did folk put the trespass and their response firmly under the carpet, so that I never saw that righteous anger at sin was godly? How did people handle anger? Did people ever get forgiven? Did anyone ever say sorry? What was the message that came through?

When I look at the cross, what is the *message* about conflict resolution? God has taken me to court at the cross. In this He has acted justly, establishing my guilt, making a public statement before the witness of all creation about His grievances against me, remarkably without specifically shaming me as an individual. He has exacted just punishment for my sin so that debt is paid in full. He has loved mercy, in that He has spent His anger for those He has called to Himself, and has put on Jesus Christ, His only Son, the guilt that is mine, and declared me innocent. I have been called to account, shown the punishment that I deserved and then offered mercy and grace. This is remarkable. The cross calls me to act justly, love mercy and offer abundant grace to both myself and others.

Since conflict is always present in fallen human relationships, intimacy is about how I relate once conflict is resolved. As I think about intimacy and fellowship in relationship, what was the message I received about this through my family tree and childhood experience? Did the big people in my life model intimacy and fellowship well (by selflessly blessing and warmly receiving the good that each has to offer)? Did they offer a picture of how Christ the lover woos and enthrals His beloved the Church? Did one lay down their life and the other respond with respect and honour? Was marriage and family relationship prized above other human interactions, such as church or work? Or was 'intimacy' portrayed through coldness and distance, or self-centred control and manipulation? What was the message that came through?

When I look at the cross, what is the *message* about intimacy? God the Father has stooped to the cross, selflessly moved towards us through Jesus His Son and has kissed me as His loved child. Jesus has paid in full the redemption fee and has also come to claim me as a vital part of His beloved bride. He has provided everything I now need to be beautiful in His sight. He is in love. In His grace, He has told us the final chapter in advance: fully known, looking at last face to face, the bride will love Him back and honour Him as He deserves. The cross woos me towards becoming the child of the Father, the beloved bride of His Son and even the temple of His Holy Spirit. Out of this all other relationships can become selflessly and warmly intimate.

Real food – real drink

The Gospels offer a window into the fellowship that Jesus experienced with His disciples and therefore into the kind of fellowship we may well experience as His people. As Jesus prepares for His own sacrifice, He first offers a physical picture of His humiliation and the preparation required to receive the blessings of that same sacrifice. He challenges us that this is the road that you and I must follow.

Perhaps I can imagine myself in the scene. As I gather around the meal with my brothers, I become aware that the host must always ensure the comfort of his guests as they recline at table. But there is no servant available. My feet itch. They feel dry and sore and the dust of the Bethany road has done its work. The jug of water and the towel have been prepared: standing to one side they deafen me with their silence. With the argument about who is the greatest among the disciples still ringing in my ears, I retreat from taking up the jug myself: *'Surely that is a servant's job? I am the Master's friend.'* I decide to ignore my feet; sure that no one will notice. After all, what does it matter? I am no different to you. Your feet are in the same state. Having sat down, none of us offers to help. Everyone is too quick to deny the problem and too proud to serve.

As a lover to His beloved, a bridegroom to His bride, Jesus then takes up His responsibility and demonstrates true leadership by stripping down to the undergarments that a slave would wear and proceeds to wash my feet. I look at Him. Do I receive or protest? He tells me that if I am to have a part in Him, I must allow Him to serve me. He assures me that I am clean enough in body to be at the table, only this simple washing is required. I watch His hands on my feet – bathing both the dust of the road and the wounds of the journey. Carefully and lovingly, I am made ready for fellowship, for intimacy with Him. And after He has washed the feet of each one, He dresses and returns to His place: *'Now that I, your Lord and Teacher, have washed your feet, you also should wash one another's feet. I have set you an example that you should do as I have done for you'* (Jn 13:14).

Having made me ready, He encourages me to do likewise, preparing every brother and sister in His bride for fellowship with Him. He is inviting me to prepare you to eat with Him, and to let you prepare me. People, He is calling us out of denial and into mutual acknowledgement of both our sin and our woundedness. He is calling us to one another. He is asking us to see the mess and be willing to clean it up. This is the body being made ready. This is Church. This is the *message*.

Still the food remains untouched. Now the moment arrives when Jesus reveals the deepest mystery: *'One of you is going to betray me'* (Jn 13:21). As Bonhoeffer says, *'His enemies cannot gain power over him alone. For that they need one of his friends… This most horrible thing occurs not from without, but from within.'*[8]

If it is His path to the cross, then there is every reason why it should also be both mine and yours. Who has betrayed me? Which friend in whom I trusted, with whom I shared my daily bread, has lifted up his heel against me and helped the enemy to gain power over me? Is it a mother, a father, a brother or sister, a spouse, a child, a colleague, a friend? Who is it that moved towards me to kiss me, yet behind my back and even unconsciously, has sold me into the hands of the enemy for their own paltry gain? And what will I do to repay them?

Jesus turns to me: *'As I have loved you, so you must love one another'* (Jn 13:34). I look at Him. How does He love me? Now, how will I love my friend who betrayed me? And so Jesus takes the bread, gives thanks for it and says, *'This is my body given for you; do this in remembrance of me'* (Lk 22:19).

How does He invite me to remember Him? Luke uses the Greek word *anamnesis*, which does not mean 'in memory of' but rather an affectionate calling to mind of the person Himself as if He physically stood before me. Remembrance in this sense is an awakening of my mind, a coming up from where I have completely forgotten Him to the glorious reality of His presence.

But as an adult in Christ, I do see Jesus in the here and now. He stands before me clear as day. It is not now that I need to remember Him, but then. Somewhere in a dim room of my memory, the child or the adolescent or even the adult I was some weeks ago aches in need. I have forgotten God there. At the very point of my unmet need, where I have fallen away from the active recollection of who He is, where I have fallen from the bright memory of the goodness of God and have experienced emptiness and wounding. Here is the place, here is the time where I must remember Him as He is.

He offers His body. As I allow Him to suffer in my place, taking the terrible impact of the fall for me, He gives me His flesh. I take it and eat. It is real food. I can receive the wholeness of the Son of God.

And so Jesus takes the cup, gives thanks for it and says, *'This cup is the new covenant in my blood, which is poured out for you'* (Lk 22:20). It is not just now that I need to access the power of His shed blood, but it is also then. In the same dim room of my memory, the child or adolescent or adult I was has sinned. Out of unmet need, where I had fallen away from that bright memory of the goodness of God, I chose my own way – independence. Here is the place, here is the time where now I must turn to Him and allow Him to take my place in both punishment and guilt, receiving into myself the cleansing of His shed blood.

His life is poured out. As I allow Him to die in my place, suffering the terrible impact of my sin, He offers me His blood. I take it. It is real drink. I can receive the innocence and righteousness of the Son of God.

In this way, Christ comes to dwell in my heart through active faith in that place where I had lost belief, giving me access to the Father as His adopted child, whole and dependent once again, receiving the blessing that Adam had lost – eternal life.

'I tell you the truth, unless you can eat the flesh of the Son of Man and drink his blood, you have no life in you. Whoever eats my flesh and drinks my blood has eternal life, and I will raise him up on the last day. For my flesh is real food and my blood is real drink' (Jn 6:53–55).

So what about the baby I once was? At what point of unmet need does Jesus long to offer Himself to me as an infant? Deep in my soul, I still long for a father who will put himself out to offer steadfast security and provision. I still long for him to take the place of a mother who seemingly cannot be trusted. Erroneously, I believe that because he seems to have abandoned me (both to the nursing home and my mother), my father does not really love me. Deep within I have concluded that I am rejectable, worthless and insignificant.

Does Jesus love the baby I was, keep her safe in His arms, provide for her needs and acknowledge her unique purpose? Although as an adult I immediately say yes, yet in my heart I do not know. That is the reaction of the baby. What I can do by faith is to take that bread into the emptiness created by being seemingly unloved and trust that the body of Christ will fill me there. By the same faith, I can also take the wine and allow His blood to cleanse me of the sin that took root at those early moments of my life. What sin? My choices made then began a route to independent living in relationship. I chose to refuse some of the good my father longed to offer me. I chose to draw out the feminine in men in order to connect with the maternal more safely than through women. I chose to protect myself from women and so avoid any further rejection. These are put upon Jesus and I am forgiven at the root, the very point that I began to sin that way. I can start again as an infant looking for the reality of His face turned towards me. Does He see me? Will He keep me safe? Will He love me?

CHAPTER 10
CHOOSING REALITY

Even as I stand at the cross and encourage the infant I once was to look upon Christ and trust in His suffering and the guilt He bears for her, still I have not quite got the *message* about God the Father as a perfect parent. I have seen the possibility of being Abba's child, but have not yet accessed Him as fully as I am able. In His severe mercy, I need the Spirit of God to come and strip me clean of all that remains of my entrenched wrong perceptions about God the Father as a provider.

Choosing reality about God and ourselves

According to God, the most significant relationship in my life is my relationship with Him. If that is true then my relational style with God deserves close scrutiny. How do I relate to a provider upon whom I am designed to be dependent? There are times when I behave as if the truth is true whether or not I believe it in my heart and independent of how I feel. For brief moments, I am willing to live on the edge of faith and serve my Lord and King as a passionate warrior in His kingdom. As I actively call Jesus to mind as the commander of the Lord's army, I tend to act as if His Father is good, holy and sovereign. In these moments I really am an adult in Christ. I rejoice as I take my part in the deliverance of God's people, whether or not I am seen and accepted by others, whatever the cost to me, however extravagant my sacrifice must be.

But is this the real me? In part, it is. I know that I am designed to be a warrior, but some of this is my way of trying to ensure that God includes me and that He sees me. Referring to the examples of relational style in Chapter 3, I am like the 'little professor' on the battlefield of kingdom living. If I push myself to be the best warrior I can be, how will God manage without me? So this is one way that I pretend with God, a mask I wear to get Him to love me.

But the warrior does not play much. In fact I do not do 'child' at all well with God. So focused on the salvation battle, I am fairly useless at relaxing and simply having fun. I have very little idea how to be a kid with my heavenly Daddy, sitting on His lap, whiling away the hours by simply being with Him, with nothing to do. When God does not want to engage my services in His kingdom, I have to admit that I feel wounded. As I nurse my hurt, I actually find myself pondering: *'Why would He want to use someone else?'* Then, with nothing to do, I usually retreat into absolute silence and isolation, acting as if there is no God at all, no warm provider who would look after my interests instead of me having to look after them myself. Seeing myself as alone in a hostile and abandoning universe, I become the definition of independence.

So who is this? By now you will recognise this as the infant in me. This is my way of ensuring that I protect myself from the rending disappointment of God not including me, rejecting me, not seeing who I am. I see myself in this position when I am not working as a warrior. I struggle to pray for others because in my heart I believe there is not a good God to pray to. I struggle to read His word, because in my heart I believe that if He exists, then God has no interest in me and no desire to communicate with me. This is definitely the worldview of the infant, alone in the nursing home.

How have I formed my relational style with God? The relationships where I learnt something good or bad about dependency were with my parents and other significant care-givers. I have simply transferred my perceptions of these care-givers straight onto Him. At a significant moment of unmet need in human relationships, what stopped me from simply turning to God as He is and receiving the fullness of His provision? Why did I choose independence and idolatry instead? Scripture tells me that at whatever age, I am without excuse. The reality is that God in His fullness has been alongside me all the time, communicating the *message*:

> *Listen to Me...you whom I have upheld since you were conceived, and have carried since your birth. Even to your old age and grey hairs: I am He, I am He who will sustain you. I have made you and will carry you; I will sustain you and I will rescue you.*
>
> Is 46:3–4

Why did I not listen? I chose independence because I like independence. It felt good to be in control because I hated being needy and dependent. Why? I hated being needy because of how I saw

God. I see that, as a child, I believed the lie that He was absent or did not care or, worse still, was dead or non-existent. These unconscious wrong perceptions of God as a provider underlie my relational style with Him.

What I actually believe about God as my spiritual provider is the most important thing about me. It literally defines me. As I see my provider, so I draw my identity from this 'god', and am moulded in its image. Some of what I believe about God is true. Out of that truth, as I see who He really is, I see who I really am (some of which is a warrior). But my relational style with God indicates that I also hold some rather different beliefs about my 'god'. He only involves me and includes me in his company if I am useful for rescuing others. In other words, he only wants me when he needs me. He is a god who is passionate about what is true. He loves the cut and thrust of battle and even enjoys the bittersweet savour of painful defeat as well the glory of victory. He is also a changeable god. A good deal of the time he acts as though I am useless to him and pays me no attention whatsoever. In this mood if he were to seek me out, I see that he is self-absorbed, an island, with no need of anyone. Strongly masculine, this 'god' is my childhood perception of my father in his relationship with me. This is not a god who plays much with me. He does not delight in rest and cuddles. I have moulded myself in his image. With such a god, it is logical to look after myself. It is logical to refuse to be vulnerable and helplessly dependent. It is logical to choose independence.

I am beginning to see that my unconscious beliefs about God have generated my feelings about Him and have directed my behaviour in relationship with Him. They are the foundation of

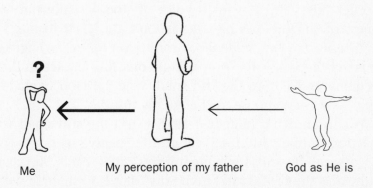

Me   My perception of my father   God as He is

my relational style both with Him and, indeed, with everyone. All the while I have believed that I have been serving God as He is, but in reality I have been serving the idol god of my parents, who is no god at all. I have missed the mark.

Like Adam and Eve before me, I have allowed my inbuilt knowledge of the goodness of God, the eternity that God has set in my heart, to become spoilt and twisted. This means that independence is inevitable. Undoing this spoiling usually takes a sustained movement of God in my life, as He graciously exposes the lies that I believe about Him and allows me to actually feel the vast emptiness within. A raging thirst swirls within me at my core. Over the years it has driven me to find relief through one defensive strategy after another. Now, finally, I need to allow that same thirst to drive me into the arms of God as He is: *'May it be the real I who speaks. May it be the real Thou that I speak to.'*[9]

There is but one place, one moment in time, when eternity has broken afresh into fallen creation and enabled me to see God clearly. All my times must now be placed deliberately into His hands nailed upon that cross, that I might gaze through Him at His Father beyond. Jesus is the image of the invisible God, the exact representation of His being, in whom God the Father was pleased to have all His fullness dwell. This means that it is Jesus I must look at to really see God the Father – not my dad nor my mum nor you, but Jesus. As I peer through the prism of His crucified body, as I listen intently to the Word that is being communicated, what sort of parent, what sort of provider do I see? What is the *message* that I hear?

I have found it invaluable to make such messages (uniquely tailored to a particular block in my thinking) simultaneously consciously heard. One friend might take the role of the enemy while the other offers the still small voice of God. Usually the reasonableness of the enemy's message is loud and clear to me. I have been listening to that same tape droning on for years. I agree with it. It is my life script. But now my unconscious choice to listen to the enemy and ignore the still small voice of God is made conscious. Now I can choose to change my mind.

As I listen, what happens? First, I find the still small voice a distraction from my intense focus on the enemy's message. The latter seems real. It seems to define my version of reality. At this point I might stop the process and invite my friends to share how it feels

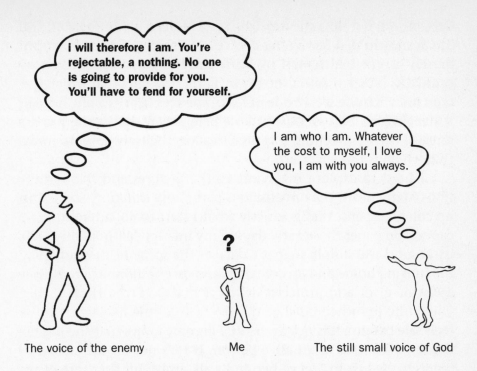

The voice of the enemy   Me   The still small voice of God

to be speaking to me in this way. Typically the person taking the role of the enemy will talk of how much power they see that their words have in my life. Probably my eyes and ears have been fixed intently upon them. Typically the person taking the role of God will talk of how sad they feel at the loss of relationship, how much they long for me to turn, look God in the eye and listen to the truth. This helps. Hearing about God's longing for me through His image-bearer triggers me into finding some power to choose God and resist the enemy.

So I start to tune in to the right direction, like fiddling with a dial on a radio. Through the work of the Holy Spirit, the eternity that God has set in my heart begins to wake up. The bright memory of being His comes afresh to a deep place in my thinking. God is calling more of me back to Himself, and remarkably after years of ignoring Him in that area, I want to respond. I begin to lean into the voice of God, longing to be held and supported by the person behind that *message*. Then I finally find the power to tell the enemy to shut up.

How does this relate to the baby I was? Her defensive structure has had a major impact upon both my relationship with God and with others. But now she has allowed Jesus into her little heart, she has acknowledged her wrong choices and she has begun to empty herself of grief. Although by faith she has eaten His body and drunk His blood, it is still mostly by faith, believing that which she does not yet quite see. Aware of Jesus, she sees Him as a brother. He is hanging on a cross; how can He parent her? As yet she has no sense of the resurrection. It is time to allow the Holy Spirit to make that which is unseen, seen.

I need to explore the symbols, the pictures and the perceptions in my heart: the unconscious part of my thinking. So, taking up coloured pens, that is exactly what I start to do, attempting to capture on paper those early days of my infancy. Without any ability at art, I use simple shapes to depict the scene in the garden of the nursing home and answer the ultimate question: where is God as a care-giver and protector when it hurts? Maybe He is in the 'blue' (the upturned bowl of the sky feels a little like a womb). It feels safe because it is not a person. I become aware that she has no desire to see Jesus as an alive person. If He's not on the cross, He seems likely just to ignore her and walk away. But there are other people in the picture, they were just absent at the time. Remarkably this absence is the powerful way they make their presence felt. Drawing in the distant figures of my parents means that I can choose to put the 'face' I have inadvertently placed onto God back onto them, where it belongs.

As I do this, how do I perceive God the Father when I look at Him through the cross? Oh there He is! The baby in my heart is genuinely surprised, because she sees that He looks like the Jesus of the Gospels, suffering the little children to come to Him. Wonderfully, He is dressed completely in blue. And in Jesus, He has arms to hold her, a chest that holds a beating heart and, best of all, a face to gaze upon. In Jesus, God the Father has the body of a parent who believes that relating is more important than working in an office.

Having been rigid with terror, with her eyes closed, now it takes time to relax in His arms. Amazingly He has always been there. Very still, He has been singing softly to her for years. Finally she is drinking in His *message* of safe acceptance. She trusts that she is seen by Him, that she is well provided for. She trusts that she is safe and loved. Her face feels the glow of His eyes constantly upon her, beaming with maternal love. Drinking in this living water,

eventually she opens her eyes and gazes transfixed as only a baby can. The sun has entered the 'blue', and remarkably, in her heart she can look upon Him and live.

At this deep level, by the grace of God, I have let Jesus in to bring His mercy, comfort and life. He is renewing my thinking by His truth, which is Himself, His presence, because truth is personified in Jesus Christ. All the intellectual reality in the world will not transform me; it has to be Him in person. So I can change my mind about God, renouncing the basic lie that He is not holy and good and that He is not up to looking after me properly. For me, in this part of my story, this is the very root of repentance: *'In this I greatly rejoice, though now for a little while I have suffered grief in this trial. This has come so that my faith – of greater worth than gold, which perishes even though refined by fire – may be proved genuine and may result in praise, glory and honour when Jesus Christ is revealed. Though I have not seen him, I love him; and even though I do not see him now, I believe in him and am filled with an inexpressible and glorious joy, for I am*

receiving the goal of my faith, the salvation of my soul.' (Adapted from
1 Pet 1:6–9.)

Jesus has come within my self-constructed 'place of safety',
the desert place in my heart where I have suffered and died, and
transformed it through His death into the garden of the resurrection. What do I discover here? There is time. There is peace. There
is beauty. This is the place where the adult, the child and the baby
I was can all meet and become one in Him. This is the place where
I can learn to play: *'I tell you the truth, unless you change and become
like little children, you will never enter the kingdom of heaven'* (Mt
18:3).

Quenching our deep thirst with living water

What kind of parent does the infant find in this garden of the resurrection? Again, because as a baby she actually needs people with
skin on, it is Jesus that ministers to her, helping her to receive the
fullness of His life and His relationship with His Father. Through
Jesus, she has full access to Abba, in all His paternal and maternal
love for her. But does she want that? The child of my past needs to
agree to be adopted and provided for by this perfect parent. He has
done everything that must be done in order to draw up the adop-
tion papers signed with the blood of Christ, but will she say 'yes'?

As I turn to the real God, what does He offer me? Whatever it
is, by the looks of it, there are no strings attached. His gift is unconditional.

It is Himself!

And even more wonderful, because I see Him as He is, I
become more like Him. I become more like the real me.

First, I become secure, bringing a deep sense of unconditional,
comforting acceptance and intimate connection with God. In
receiving Him, I see myself more clearly: *'Because I am unconditionally accepted, I am secure and can safely come into existence.'*

I also become worth while, bringing a deep sense of my value
to God, and His great pleasure in me, so that I am free to fully
develop. Again, in receiving still more of Him, I see myself even
more clearly: *'Because I am valued beyond measure, I am worth while
and can become myself.'*

Lastly I become significant, bringing a deep sense of God's particular purpose for my life. He is therefore I am too! But who am I? *'Because I am recognised as uniquely significant, I can be myself, the irreplaceable person that God has called me to be.'*

In allowing God to reveal His reality to me through Christ, I have found myself receiving a heart-held, scriptural image, feeding me at a pace that I can cope with in some of the deep and hungry places of my body, soul and spirit. We dance. Just for now we are not at war and the sword and the armour can wait. I see that He tenderly holds the baby I was. The maternal heart of the Father is beating deep within His chest and smiling through His eyes. Amazing miracle, she is beginning to smile! Yes, I am made for war, but I am also made for love, to be enjoyed by my loving Creator and to enjoy Him in return. As an adult in Christ I knew of this place and believed it to be true, but I had only visited it to be still and recover from the wounds of battle, not to play or dance or laugh. Never before had I stayed to rest simply for the sake of enjoying that rest. Why not? Because never before had I brought the baby with me. *'Whoever drinks the water I give him will never thirst. Indeed, the water I give him will become in him a spring of water welling up to eternal life'* (Jn 4:14).

As the infant of my past is loosened from the lies under which I have lived, now as an adult I need to discipline myself to focus and feed upon reality – the *message* about who God is, who I am, and the relationship between the two. I need to practise living out of this truth on a moment-by-moment basis: *'You were taught, with regard to your former way of life, to put off the old self, which is being corrupted by its deceitful desires; to be made new in the attitude of your minds; and to put on the new self, created to be like God in true right-eousness and holiness'* (Eph 4:22–24).

What is His *message* to me, and who is the new self?

> *I am the Father. You are my child.*
> *I am the Lover. You are my beloved.*
> *I am the Spirit. You are my temple.*

This is what it means for Yahweh to be our God and for you and I to be His people. Individually and corporately we are His new cre-ation. As dependent children of our Father, we are affirmed as uniquely purposeful individuals. As part of the bride of Christ, we are affirmed as diverse members of a new community with its own culture, and whom one day, Jesus will come and partner for ever. As His physical temple, we are affirmed as His dwelling place. He wants to make His home in us, in our flesh, for ever. Then the dwelling of God will be with men, with all our longings (parental and peer) fulfilled in God eternally: *'There will be no more death or mourning or crying or pain, for the old order of things has passed away'* (Rev 21:4).

You and I tasted the fruit of the knowledge of good and evil, and in an immediate physical and spiritual sense we died, just as God said we would. Yet in the context of God's mysterious, larger story, the paradigm that Satan offered in Genesis 3 is bizarrely true: Adam's seed would not die, our eyes would be opened and we would indeed become like God, knowing good and evil. It is how we personally interpreted this larger truth, in a way that doubted our unseen God, that caused the fall and continues to blight us now. But through Jesus' trust in the invisible God and the faith He plants in our hearts, somehow we are now being made alive in Christ. We are being transformed into His likeness, becoming untainted by the knowledge of good and evil, able in spite of it to responsively and selflessly love. In this way, as the apostle Peter says, you and I will finally participate in the divine nature, able to know good and evil and yet remain thoroughly good. Only by the enormity of divine grace will we have escaped the corruption of evil. This is the reason God allowed the fall and is redeeming us in the way He does. This is the only way we would come, as individuals and as a community of faith, to trust that He is good. This is the way we grow up. This is His way of making us, His unworthy creatures, to be like Him: one in community together.

So what about me right now? As I repent more deeply, day by day, and believe the good news that I am loved, I become free to cleave to God as I should and truly find my Sabbath rest in Him. In this way, I allow God more and more to come into that very thirsty place at the core of my being, bringing His living water which will stream up and out of me into creation. Thus will I proclaim and become the *message* that I was always intended to be.

And what of the false self that may still remain? You know, the bit that still raises its ugly head and seeks to get rather than give; the part that would rather skulk about in a half-existence, seeking to protect itself from disappointment rather than receive? Does God intend my real self to be gracious to that part or to crucify it?

Should I suffer it as an inevitable part of being incompletely sanctified or put it off completely like an old coat? I believe that God intends me to hold each opposite attitude in tension. On the one hand, as the apostle Paul says, I am to put off the old self. On the other hand, I am encouraged to offer grace and acceptance without encouraging sin.

As God lovingly pursues me and seeks to reconcile me to Himself, the restoration process will have its inevitable ups and downs. I do need to learn to accept God and His perfectly timed restoration plan for my life. As He does with all creation, God tends to reveal Himself to me in a progressive and cumulative manner. Because I was made for perfection, I long for it now. But to be like God, to adequately communicate the *message*, I need to patiently allow all things to come to completion in Him. He is the perfect parent, who neither rushes His children to the altar to wed His Son while they are still in nappies, nor overprotectively holds them back from the maturation process through the impact of the fall.

Thus in accepting God and His plan, I must also accept the fall, which although not His desired will for me, is certainly something He has permitted. Although He hates it, in many ways even God accepts the fall in that He works with it; it is redeemable. In all this I can allow my longing for perfection to motivate me towards deeper dependency upon God while still allowing myself to suffer some tumbles and scraped knees and learn perseverance along the way: *'But we also rejoice in our sufferings, because we know that suffering produces perseverance; perseverance, character; and character, hope. And hope does not disappoint us, because God has poured out his love into our hearts by the Holy Spirit, whom he has given us'* (Rom 5:3–5).

I also need to accept myself and my currently imperfect ways of receiving all that He perfectly offers. Biblically, I am called to rejoice in my real self (the image bearer), love my wounded self (the empty part, wounded by the fall) and crucify the false self (the agent of sin). It can be confusing to separate out these different aspects. One useful tool is to apply the wisdom of the Holy Spirit in naming the different parts. Scripturally, naming gives me authority, particularly over the false part of me.

Roselyn (literally, *'beautiful rose'*) – the real me, the image-bearer, the 'poiema'; an infant of some weeks in age, learning to gurgle and smile, relating warmly to people; also a warrior adult, beloved by her captain, Christ.

Little Ros – the wounded me: an infant of some weeks old, hungry for warm physical connection from a parental figure.

Island – the false me, the mask, the agent of sin; the independent choices of the infant; isolation; rejection and hatred of others.

Some would say that *Island* has served me well as an infant, that without this defence, the shock of my mother's unpredictable behaviour and the perceived physical and emotional rejection would have had a far worse effect in my life. But God has called this defensive independence sin, so how can it have served me well? I see the fruit of this defence as short-term comfort, loneliness, a childhood refusal to receive from my mother, a well-hidden hatred of others, strongly ambivalent reactions to relationship with my father, emotional dependent reactions towards other women in adolescence and adult life, and much more that is harmful both to myself and others. While I find *Island* understandable, I do not find this part excusable. I believe that Scripture exhorts me to crucify these choices. As I do this with God, I see that *Island* does not go easily. She has many things to say about others, how bad they are, how threatening they can be. But, continually taking authority over that part of myself, she simply must continue to go in the name of Jesus, along with everything of the enemy that has made its home in her.

What about *Little Ros*? This is the broken part of my being that both needs and deserves tender compassion and abundant grace. It will take time to learn to receive from God. The real adult self is only just learning to lay down her sword and become a foster mother to this baby, taking her to God in all His paternal and maternal love, to ensure that she receives all that she has so long needed: *'Can a mother forget the baby at her breast and have no compassion on the child she has borne? Though she may forget, I will not forget you! See, I have engraved you on the palms of my hands'* (Is 49:15–16).

'For you did not receive a spirit that makes you a slave again to fear,

but you received the Spirit of sonship. And by Him we cry, "Abba, Father." The Spirit himself testifies with our spirit that we are God's children' (Rom 8:15–16).

'Though my mother and father forsake me, the LORD will receive me... I am still confident of this: I will see the goodness of the LORD in the land of the living' (Ps 27:10–13).

Finally, I also need to accept others. As I accept the world as fallen and finite, I come face to face with the disappointment that there is never going to be a human parent to come along, sort me out and perfectly communicate the *message*. In a fallen world, other than God, no one else can meet my deep needs and I am essentially alone. This does not mean that God does not often use folk to transmit His *message* of familial love. After all, that is what we are here for, particularly when we are parents.

Now that my own parents have gone beyond my human grasp into the hands of our compassionate and gracious God, I look back and see that sometimes ours was a difficult journey together. But not for one moment do I regret taking it with them. The infant in my heart can accept and honour her father in his passion to bring order out of chaos through purposeful work, and in his longing to provide well and keep hunger and homelessness at bay. She can also honour her mother, who despite her mental illness, returned from hospital to relate warmly with me as a baby, offering a few good years of fun-filled maternal affection. Together, despite their imperfections, in their warmth and in their passion they communicated something of the *message*. I hope I did too.

But how am I to see and relate to other people in my world?

CHAPTER 11
LIVING IN REALITY

It may help at this point to remind myself where I was in the beginning. According to the first letter of John, if I claim intimacy with God I need to 'walk my talk' and choose to be vulnerably real with Him. The unexpected benefit of this is that I will mature sufficiently to be vulnerably real with you too. Rather than always seeking that you parent me (whether you are an individual or a people group such as church or the government), I could learn to be your peer. To do this I need to acknowledge and rebuke the lies that I have foolishly believed about you and instead proclaim and live out of the truth. This is all part of the repentance process, as I learn to love you as you are, rather than hate you because of how I have judged you to be. The quality of our fellowship together will bring the *message* home and is how God's love is made complete in us as His people.

Choosing reality about others

As I have allowed Jesus to enter into and clear up my internal messiness that was hidden behind the mask of my relational style, some of my false perceptions of people have risen like dross to the surface of a crucible. I see that I tend to judge certain groups of people, such as men, women, authority figures, peers, family, dependants, church, medics, teachers, particular ethnic or cultural groups, political or religious parties, and so on. You name a group and both you and I will discover that we probably have prejudicial opinions about them. It may not be all the folk in a certain category, but only those with certain attitudes or relational styles or in certain contexts and settings.

For example, the Christian neighbour who constantly offers his solution as the right one, not respecting my own autonomy or abilities may unconsciously remind me of a controlling authority figure from my childhood. The silence of a church leader amid relational problems in the congregation may forcibly remind you of passivity in parental figures when, as a little child, you yearned for practical, loving involvement and protection. The peers at work who most regularly form 'cliques', cutting folk out of the loop of fellowship may remind us all of the playground gang leaders who seemed to have absolute authority to include or exclude. Certainly, following the story of the infant of my past, I tend to have stronger prejudicial reactions towards women who seem to criticise without cause or men who seem to fail to protect me from apparent relational harm, or worse still ignore me all together.

I find myself increasingly frustrated with my prejudices against others. Perhaps now it is time to re-educate myself? After all, if the child in me is truly loved by the Father and if, as an adult, I am Christ's beloved, why must you continue to come through for me at all? The answer is that there is no longer any 'must'. In Christ the demand has gone. It is wonderful if you do communicate the *message*, but it is OK, although sad, if you do not. The loss of the 'must' means that I no longer hate you or find myself indifferent to you, or remain withdrawn and aloof from you. Instead, I long to relate.

The dictionary tells me that ambivalence is the co-existence of opposing emotional attitudes towards the same object. Ambivalence is at the root of the fallen human condition. I both love and hate the object of my desire when it cannot or will not fulfil me. But you do not deserve my ambivalence towards you for you never were designed to be my god. You never were meant to be my 'all in all'. My ambivalent attitude towards you needs to be acknowledged, repented of, rightly sourced and dealt with before the cross. By rightly sourcing my ambivalence, I mean that I allow God to help me access the root relational problems that led to this attitude in relationships.

Take another typical example. Perhaps a female friend rather emotionally 'bends my ear', seemingly without reason. I would see myself as innocent and unjustifiably blamed. That would be bad enough but perhaps her criticism is volleyed over the net like a Wimbledon ace with some very forcible emotions. Unlike myself, she seems unafraid to express her very strong feelings. As I attempt to defend myself, I find I am both angry and hurt, but express little of this directly. Away from the one-to-one contact, I briefly fantasise about withdrawing from the relationship all together. Internally my self-talk is fuelled by my anger: I despise her lack of emotional self-control. I hate her selfishness. She has put her own needs before my own. I want to bin the friendship because if I stay in it she is likely to shred me. I hate her. I think that emotionally expressive, critical women are 'the pits'! And so on.

At the very same time, I feel compassion for my friend, who is perhaps having a rough time at home or at work. I long for unity between us and feel the strength of my commitment in befriending her. Although her behaviour is not excusable, I see that amid her personal circumstances, her resources for other-centeredness are at a low ebb. I think about the times we have enjoyed each other's company. I love her. I think my friend is fallen but OK. From her real self, she ministers Christ to me.

What is all this about? My reaction is only slightly about my friend. Most of it is about my mother. Once again I am predominantly relating to my friend, not as an adult, but as a needy child. The infant in my soul is remembering my mother's poor reactions towards me, heavily charged by the chaotic emotions of mental breakdown. But it is God who will provide for me as a needy child, not my friend. As I once again allow Father God to hold that early moment in time in His hand, I invite the cross to pierce through into my loneliness there. This is mainly where my hurt and anger belong. And this is where I must express it.

I need to deliberately verbally renounce and refuse any inner lies that I have believed about my friend, binding them into the cross. My friend is not 'the pits'. Some of her reactions are unhelpful. Perhaps I do need to challenge her to think before she speaks. She, and other women who may exhibit similar reactions, are neither out to get me, abuse me nor destroy me. In Christ, I will survive. Likewise, I am not as innocent as I make out. But I am OK and so is she.

'Do not conform any longer to the pattern of this world, but be transformed by the renewing of your mind' (Rom 12:2). Day by day, if I am to communicate the *message* to my friend, offering her the fruit of the Spirit in my life, I need to live out of the truth about who she is: a fallen creature not the creator, unable to meet my needs completely, not necessarily out to 'get' or reject me, not there for me to use, abuse or ignore. She and I are designed to relate with one another. I had better get on with my part.

Suppose a maternal figure came to me and seriously apologised about the impact of the irrational, emotional outbursts of mothers towards children. Suppose she acknowledged before God maternal responsibility: that there are times when mothers have chosen to dump their feelings on their kids rather than consider how to handle emotions in other ways? Suppose, as a mother, she said sorry for the hurt mothers had inflicted on their kids? Suppose she clearly longed for mothers to change and to make amends? What would that feel like to me?

Since no one has ever done that, I can only speculate. But as I imagine it in my mind, I see that it is clearly not my mother apologising. That is between her, me and God. But it is a representative person saying sorry. This woman cannot and must not say my mother's 'sorrys'. But her surrogate repentance does open a long-bolted door for me. It softens my heart. In my mind's eye, I suddenly see access between myself and women reacting similarly to my mother. I can forgive them. I see myself walking towards them, not with an angry demand, but a loving desire to relate.

But this also stimulates within me a confession and apology that I must make, both personal and representative: *'I want to speak to all mothers and maternal figures. I speak to you as a child who has now grown into a woman and into a mother herself. I speak to you as a child who has shut you out. Women, where you have been emotionally irrational and critical with me, where you have blamed me and I thought myself innocent, where you have dumped your emotional baggage onto me, I have hated you. I have refused relationship with you to the extent that I would not even receive the good I knew that you have had to offer. I want to say that 'dumping emotions' is not OK, neither in me, nor in you. Shutting out is not OK either. These things must be challenged in our relationship with one another. Whether you choose to change or not, I am sorry for my part, that I have shut you out and refused all that you have to offer me. Please forgive me.*

'Please also forgive the children in your own lives who have treated you this way – the kids who have shut you out and failed to honour you as God intends. We have sinned against you. Whatever your faults, you are mothers to us, a gift from God. I rejoice in all the ways that you reflect the maternal heart of the Father. Thank you for your mother's love, for your mother's heart. Whatever the mistakes, whatever the faults on both sides, I want to celebrate your role in our lives.'

Representational apology like this is incredibly powerful. Here I am identifying with a particular group of people who have sinned in a certain way. As a member of that group, I stand in the gap before God and before others, confess our collective sin and say sorry. And God does the rest of the work that is appropriate at that level. Influenced by the secular culture around us, western evangelicals tend to prize individuality at the expense of group. We focus on the responsibility of the individual to confess and repent, and tend to underplay the sinful impact of groups of people, both currently and historically. But biblical prophets, priests and kings were individuals called to stand in the gap and identify with a particular people group, both before God and before others. Each acknowledged the sin of the group and acted as an intercessor, pleading for mercy. Through His death on the cross, Jesus is the prime example of this kind of personal representative, even teaching us to individually and collectively pray in the same way: *'Our Father... give us this day... forgive us our sins as we forgive... lead us not... deliver us... '* and so on. As I pray this prayer I cannot help but feel a 'group' around me. I stand in the gap for my family, my local community, my nation, my culture, and even for the human race.

So now if you and I aim to individually represent genuine repentance from one people group to another, God breaks the barriers in our thinking and hearts where we have judged and written off whole sections of society or even Church itself. In my role as a counsellor, I have found that representational apology from church leadership, church flock, medics, teachers, pupils, lawyers, politicians, mothers, fathers, siblings, children, particular cultures or races, etc. are all helpful where there has been a history of neglect or abuse. Suddenly the paths to the body of Christ are opened again.

Putting on the mind of Christ

For though we live in the world, we do not wage war as the world does. The weapons we fight with are not the weapons of the world. On the contrary, they have divine power to demolish strongholds. We demolish arguments and every pretension that sets itself up against the knowledge of God, and we take captive every thought and make it obedient to Christ.

(2 Cor 10:3–5)

There is divine power at my disposal in the battle to recondition my thinking so that it conforms to the mind of Christ. As a warrior in combat, I am given a powerful weapon to wield against every thought, every internal argument at odds with God's view of reality. When applied to the root where I learnt a lie, Scripture will demolish my inner stronghold of distorted reality. (Much like pruning roses, you need to cut back the weak and diseased stems from the point where they started, otherwise they continue to grow season after season.) Like all trainee warriors, I need to approach my lessons and the battle itself with a certain amount of vigour and energy, taking authority over the lies I have believed. As my self-awareness develops I learn to observe my emotional or behavioural reactions, and so my muddled version of reality begins to be exposed to the judgement bar of Scripture:

> **A** = an experience
> **B** = my underlying belief about **A**
> **C** = my subsequent emotion and consequent behaviour
> **D** = dispute (questioning of **B** in the light of Scripture)
> **E** = effective new belief (scriptural replacement to **B**)

From my example above:

C = my subsequent anger and my consequent demand to withdraw from my friend.

A = my experience of blame being unjustly 'dumped' onto me.

B = If you unjustly dump blame onto me, I must be worthless to you. You haven't put my needs before your own, nor thought it through first in order to relate well to me. Being worthless in your eyes makes me worthless as a person.

Now I can start to dispute this:

D = This **B** that I believe is junk. Even if my friend is sometimes self-centred, that does not make me worthless (either in the eyes of her real self or universally).

To deal effectively with my underlying belief, I need to find the root of this lie. Turning my mind back to the days of my infancy, I see that the losses in my early life experience stimulated my hunger for selfless love. The infant in my heart looks upon the face of my mother and longs for some act of maternal kindness that has me as the centre not her. I see that what I experienced as the self-centredness of my mother's mental illness has left me with the deeply held conviction of my own worthlessness. From within the landscape of my heart, both the infant and the adult look longingly at Jesus. Each in our own way, we wonder: *'Will you provide for me, not counting the cost?'*

Like the apostle John, who lived out of the blessing of the name 'the disciple whom Jesus loved', in my mind's eye both the infant and the adult now readily rest their heads against the breast of Christ. I am remembering the cross and bleeding into Him a little more of my pain. The adult bleeds only slightly. She loves her friend and, in this place, does not need her love to be returned. The baby is remembering what it is like to be very vulnerable and needy with so much (seemingly) self-centred focus in the adults around her. But here with the maternal heart of Father God bleeding through the hands of His Son, she is able to rest in His sacrifice alone. His mothering is enough. Again she hears Him whisper: *'Can a mother forget the baby at her breast and have no compassion on the child she has borne? Though she may forget, I will not forget you! See, I have engraved* you *on the palms of my hands'* (Is 49:15–16).

So, having cut the lie at the root, I need to replace it with His truth:

E = I am worth providing well for. God is my provider. He has counted me worthy of His perfect, selfless provision for every moment of every day, for the whole of my eternal life with Him. *'See, can you see? He does not forget me! It is not my* name *engraved on the palms of His hands but* me, *imprinted onto Him for ever.'*

While my friend is in her own place of turmoil, I can offer her this same *message*, not forgetting her needs yet gently challenging her reactions, giving His compassionate love rather than seeking to get. In this way, through depending upon God for my needs in an attitude of humility, I begin to see her as 'better' or more important than myself, looking to her interests as well as my own.

This is the fruit of the Spirit. This is the *message*.

CHAPTER 12
STAYING REAL

A good many years ago now I was baptised by immersion in water into the community of Jesus Christ. That symbolic and sacramental act described the process of His salvation in me. At His invitation, I started the journey of dying to self, allowing the Holy Spirit to raise me to life in Christ. It was and is a joint venture. Of course, several years on I am still walking that out with varying degrees of success. As I continue to put to death the fruit of independence, facing my own sin and wounds at the cross, gradually I become more real, more like the 'little Christ' (or Christian) I am called to be, one of His people communicating the *message*, the fruit of the Holy Spirit.

So, if He is my God then, practically, how am I meant to be one of His people?

'*Hear, O Israel, the Lord our God, the Lord is one. Love the Lord your God with all your heart and with all your soul and with all your mind and with all your strength... Love your neighbour as yourself*' (Mk 12:29–31).

As Jesus sums up God's covenant expectations with these commands, Scripture uses the Greek word *agape* for love, an action word rather than an emotion. *Agape* is the highest and noblest form of love that sees something infinitely precious in its object. It describes an attitude of heart that can be recognised only by the completely unselfish actions it prompts, selflessly blessing and seeking the highest good of another. *Agape* actually cannot be defined outside the New Testament understanding of the selfless actions of almighty God towards His creation. It is a word used in a solely Christian context. It is the Christian ideal, defined perfectly by the death of Jesus Christ while we were all still sinners.

As I think about that, I hear the words of Jesus reinstating the apostle Peter but this time directed towards me: '*Ros, do you* agape *me?*' In other words: '*As I have loved you, do you love Me? As I have laid down My life to bless you, will you lay down your life to bless Me?*' Like Peter, I am forced to admit that the best I usually offer Jesus is brotherly love. As G.K. Chesterton said: '*The Christian ideal has not been tried and found wanting. It has been found difficult and left untried.*'[10]

God's purpose in His relationship with creation is to glorify or reveal Himself that we might know Him as He is. He does this through the action of *agape*. In the same way, my purpose in relationship is to glorify or reveal God. As one of His people, I am to do this through the action of *agape*. This must be my goal in relationship. Since God is the only source of *agape*, as His creature I simply do not have it in me by myself to love others that way. My love for Him and my love for you springs completely from my receptivity to His *agape* love for me: *'No longer is life to be defined by individual happiness and fulfilment, but by service; no longer by individual rights leading to alienation, but by self-emptying leading to reconciliation. The model? In Christ, God was reconciling the world to himself, not counting men's sins against them.'*[11]

Not only is community called to selflessly serve the needs of the individual but the individual is called to selflessly serve the needs of community. This is the economy of trinitarian relationship. If the *agape* of God is seen fully in the cross (selfless suffering for the sake of all others, ultimately bringing life and resurrection for both the receivers and the givers), then how do I do this in practice? As I am reconciled to God through Christ, I can choose to minister reconciliation to you through self-emptying and service, not counting your sins against you. As a 'little Christ', remarkably God is making His appeal through me: *'As you would love yourself, love your neighbour. As you would seek your own highest good, seek the highest good of your neighbour. Be the* message.'

But I am so corrupted by the fall that the only way that is going to work is for me to literally put on Christ: to clothe my heart with His heart, set my soul at one with His, place my mind at the centre of His mind and take His strength as my own.

Clothing my heart with the heart of Christ

Practically speaking, I need to set godly goals in relationship (both long term and short term) and then choose godly behaviour to achieve those goals. In each interaction I must model my choices on Christ, clothing my heart with His and asking myself the question: *What would Jesus choose?*

This all sounds very spiritual and right but the point is, in practice, *what would I choose?* In my relationship with God, I have discovered that some of my choices are about independent refusal rather than dependent trust. Now that those previously unconscious choices are conscious, I can choose instead to more readily receive from God and so honour Him as my source and sustainer. This really needs to be my life goal in relationship with God. After all, independence actually only offers me short-term gain and predictably results in long-term pain. But in Christ I can develop a lifestyle of daily repentance and intimacy with God whom I do not see. There may be short-term pain in this as I give up my usual 'gods' but there will be long-term gain. As I drink in all that He offers, I will come to truly delight in my God, blessing Him with heart-felt worship.

Although I can set this goal now and any time in prayer, what does it mean in practice? I need to learn the lost art of self-discipline. I need short-term goals, specifically SMART goals, to help me take little steps towards change, remaining accountable to others who will be prepared to offer me both support and challenge.

As I have mentioned before, a SMART goal is specific, measurable, achievable realistic and time boundaried. In my relationship with God, what SMART goals can I set? Looking back at the work He and I have done as I have been writing, there are clearly two parts of me that are in touch with their hunger for God: the adult and the infant. The adult, who is a tired but excited warrior on the battlefield, also longs to rest and enjoy being the beloved of Christ. The infant needs a mother or at least a father with a maternal heart. So, I am choosing to set the following goals:

1.   **Goal:** starting from today, for the next month, for at least ten minutes per day, I will relate as an adult with Jesus within the 'landscape of my heart'. In that time, I will resist the temptation to even discuss with Him other activity, other parts of me or the circumstances of others. We will not even read Scripture together or use a contemplative prayer book. It is simply our time to be face to face, teaching me to rest, listen, communicate lovingly and enjoy both His company and my own.

2.   **Goal:** starting from today, for the next month, for at least ten minutes per day, I will relate as an infant with Father God in all His maternal love for me within the 'landscape of my heart'. In that time, I will resist the temptation to relate in

other ways, but simply learn to rest in Him, receive from Him, to suckle at the divine breast, drinking in all the goodness of His love, filling me up on the inside. If blocks emerge then I commit to taking further time to process these at the cross. These ten minutes per day are to help the baby practise receiving.

With each of these goals, I am quite specific about what I aim to achieve. I can measure each day whether or not I have achieved the goal. They are both achievable goals for me currently, providing any blocks that emerge are worked on concurrently. It is realistic for me to set a total of only twenty minutes aside for contemplative work. Some days it may be a little longer, others not. I have also set time boundaries with a start date and a finish date, and timing for each day. These are SMART goals! Knowing my capacity to be lazy and resistant, I will need some accountability, say on a weekly basis, with a friend to whom I give full permission to directly challenge me. Without this help, I know that I will give up and fail. For me, the support and accountability of a friend is probably the most important part of the process.

In the same way, exercising my God-given freedom of choice, I can change my relational goal with others from getting (short-term gain, long-term pain) to selflessly giving (short-term pain, long-term gain). Because God is for me, I can refuse self-centredness in relationship, and choose appropriate, loving involvement with others, developing healthy boundaries, communicating both support and challenge.

I can choose to warmly receive the good lovingly offered by another (using wisdom but inspite of any disappointment about the imperfection of relationship this side of heaven). For the joy set before me, I can choose to bestow blessing through deferring gratification of my own needs and begin to boldly and lovingly give of myself to others (using wisdom but independent of the potential reception).

And so I return to my starting point: *'I want to know Christ and the power of his resurrection and the fellowship of sharing in his sufferings, becoming like him in his death, and so somehow to attain to the resurrection from the dead...I press on to take hold of that for which Christ Jesus took hold of me'* (Phil 3:10–12).

This is *agape*, to become like Christ in His death as I relate to others. As I consider this in the privacy of my office as I write, it seems noble and right, but then I go right out and start relating with someone and all my good intentions fall apart.

Agape is a long-term life goal in my relationship with others. Although I can set this goal both now and any time in prayer, how can I do it in practice? I need short-term SMART goals here as well, to help me take little steps towards change, remaining accountable to others who will be prepared to offer me both support and challenge.

In my relationship with others, what SMART goal can I set? The adult in me is sick of the isolation and loneliness that the infant has imposed through her choice to mistrust. I want to learn to be more receptive to social friendship with family and friends, but in particular with other women. I want to have fun, to enjoy as well as serve, to play as well as work. So I am choosing to set the following goals:

3. **Goal:** once a month, for the next six months, I will socialise with various female friends. During that social time, I will resist the temptation to discuss work. It will be our time together to simply enjoy one another's company.

4. **Goal:** my birthday is in a few weeks time. This year I would like to gladly welcome those who wish to celebrate my existence with me. Rather than going away on holiday to avoid it and constantly trying to minimise the event, I will choose to receive and enjoy the attention of others (particularly women) who would like to celebrate my birthday.

With each of these goals, I am quite specific about what I aim to achieve and when. Each goal is measurable and realistically achievable. Again these are SMART goals! Yet again I will need some accountability from a friend, to keep me focused, say twice over a six-month period. Support and accountability are vital if I am to change because on my own I tend to give up.

Does goal-setting work in practice? Much like new year's resolutions, when I set goals and fail, I feel miserable and tend to give up moving forward for a while. But when I set goals and achieve them, because like God I am goal-orientated, I feel great! Both God and I experience real joy when something positive is achieved, either for me or someone else. Logic and experience tell me that it is sensible to set easily achievable goals fairly often, to spur me on, because the misery of failure sets me back a hundred paces. Discipleship is a lot like dieting. Take it slow and steady in small stages, rather than aiming to get it all sorted in a week!

This system works because I believe it reflects something of God's system with us. He has not rushed to put things right for planet Earth. Because He knows our feeble frames very well, He tenderly encourages us to make tiny steps towards Him personally, as a community and generationally throughout history. He works with His people rather like a mum and dad helping junior to take his first steps. Falling on our bottom every now and then is OK, so is clinging onto the couch or mum's hand, and so is diving head first into dad's arms at the other side of the room. It is you and I that expect to make ourselves immediately race a marathon before we can even walk.

Over the last few years, I have taken both personal goal-setting and peer accountability very seriously. The result has been change. I am different to how I was back then. I relate differently to God, and I certainly relate differently with others. Finally, although the process is slow, I am growing up.

Some of the most important and impacting choices that I have made in relationship are those that have to do with communication. Sometimes I might choose to listen well to you. Other times I might not. One day, you might choose to trash my point of view. Another day, you might not. These choices matter because communication is at the very heart of relationship. Good communication builds up relationship. Poor communication tears it down.

Communication is, after all, God's way of relating. His word is spoken and creation comes into being, ready to relate to God. He speaks again and we are cursed, driven from His presence. He then sends His word to us in various ways and finally the Word Himself arrives, communicating the Father in full, drawing us back into relationship. Since then He has not stopped talking through the Word made flesh in folk like you and me. And He will send His Word again in order to finally end this part of the process. Graciously initiated by God in the first place, talking is just God's way.

The complexity and prophetic power of human speech is a core part of my image-bearing. My choices about communication shout loudly about how much or little I love others. I am a little 'word', just as I am a little Christ. In the same way that God covenants specifically with us as He relates to us as His chosen people, so it does you and I no harm to be quite specific about how we will communicate to one another in a way that glorifies God, broadcasting the *message* and so loving one another as we love ourselves.

Perhaps then it would help if we were clearer about our expectations of one another as we seek to communicate? As in any part of our relationship, our communication needs to comply with the covenant we have with each other in Christ:

You and I are in a relationship that I value and want to keep. As individuals bearing God's image, our deep needs are designed to be met primarily in God. But it is not good for either of us to be alone. God intends us to desire and experience secure love, self-worth and significant impact in relationship with each other. To this end, I choose to encourage, bless and challenge you in the following ways:

I choose to actively listen with genuine acceptance to your view about your needs. Please offer me the opportunity to clearly express my view about my needs, with your active attention and acceptance.

I choose to respect your insights, beliefs and values. Please respect mine.

I choose to risk telling you how I feel, and to be vulnerably real with you. I ask that you risk that too.

I choose to make every effort to avoid playing games with you by being unduly defensive or distorting any differences between us. I ask for your honest view of these differences.

I will try to 'sit where you sit' and understand your position as well as my own. Please do the same for me.

I will make every effort to objectively consider your observations on how you experience me in relationship. Please do the same for me.

I choose to stay open to you and work at improving our communication and relationship. Please stay open to me as we work it through together. I want a win-win outcome, not a win-lose for either of us. I want you to want the same.

What impact would it have on my relationship with you if we were to openly commit to communicate in this way? As David Augsburger says in his book of the same name, we would be 'caring enough to confront', facing into and resolving conflict in order to pursue intimacy. This is the nature of God's communication with us through the cross. In His economy, there can be no intimacy without conflict.

Setting my soul at one with Him

Self-centred behaviour reduces the possibility of experiencing uncomfortable emotions. Like you, I have spent a lifetime avoiding all kinds of uncomfortable feelings like anxiety, anger, guilt and shame. So what happens if I start to rule appropriately over my self and choose to behave differently anyway? If I were to start to be other-centred not self-centred, then what would I feel? Undoubtedly it would be something uncomfortable. So what shall I do? I could immediately choose to retreat from other-centred behaviour in order to stop that feeling. My discomfort immediately acts as a block to my SMART goal.

What would I feel? I feel nervous at the thought of making myself vulnerable and simply receiving from God and being sociable with female friends. But when I think about allowing others to celebrate my birthday, I begin to feel real anxiety. At some level, I really do not want to do it. Inwardly I steel myself, as if I expect some huge hurt to arise from the event. This is what I am avoiding when I have previously resisted celebrating my birthday with others: the anticipation of pain.

What would Jesus feel? I have to remind myself that, however crazy it seems, it is good for me to face and feel uncomfortable emotions rather than continue to deny or repress them. As I begin this process I need to rightly source my feelings, rather than aim them at innocent people including myself. As I express my emotions into the wounds of Jesus, I surrender to His solution to my problem rather than mine.

In practice, given the goals I have set myself, this means that I need to be willing to face the anxiety at the core of my soul. I think this comes from the newborn infant (so no wonder my birthday is a problem). From her perspective, immediately after her birth, she is vulnerable in relationship with her mother, hurt in the process through mum's unhelpful behaviour, and finally sent out into isolation for what feels like an eternity. I need to root this anxiety in that part of my history rather than aiming it wrongly at Jesus and my friends, particularly women. What I feel is actually very real and legitimate in the right context. So instead of avoiding my birthday, I move towards my goal. As I do so, my feelings rise to the surface to be expressed rightly this time.

Placing my mind at the centre of His mind

Through making other-centred choices, I feel disturbing emotions that I have previously avoided. As I allow myself to feel these uncomfortable emotions, I begin to expose my underlying misbeliefs about God, about myself and about others. These act as the second and more fundamental block to my SMART goal about receiving from God or others:

What would I think? Without another activity to capture your attention away from me, I am out of control and will have to be vulnerable and receptive to anything you have to offer. You will see who I am and hurt me badly because I am flawed and so unacceptable to you and everyone else. I'm not OK.

There is a great deal of wrong thinking here about God, others and myself. An underlying belief like this creates panic and even dread at the thought of simply being with someone else face to face, with nothing else for them to do but give to me. Taking each thought captive and making it obedient to Christ, I need to choose to fundamentally change my mind about where life is to be found and develop a heart-felt faith in almighty God, actively telling myself the truth.

What would Jesus think? God's attention is upon me whether or not we are actively doing something together or just being with one another. He knows who I am and loves me anyway through Jesus Christ. In Christ I am acceptable and OK.

Being vulnerable and receptive with others, particularly women, means they will see who I am and may love me well or dislike what they see. They may hurt me or they may not. Whether they like me or not, hurt me or not, this does not define me because in Christ I am acceptable to God. In Christ, I'm OK.

As the infant that I carry in my soul begins to see God aright, the same right thinking produces appropriate emotions in relationship. She tends to trust Him far more easily than she does other people. But she remains concerned about the reactions of other adults. In a fallen world, it is actually reasonable to feel concern. Along with joy, awe, righteous anger, fear of God, legitimate shame, legitimate guilt, disappointment and grief, these emotions are easily faced and felt and even lovingly expressed in the context of relationship, bringing a right and vulnerable intimacy. As I place my mind at the centre of His mind, I begin to think what Jesus thinks. And so I begin to set my soul at one with His, feeling what He feels.

Taking His strength as my own

Expressing emotions rightly leads to increased physical health, as I cease to repress my pain into my body. I need to remember that God actually likes the physical realm since He calls it good and wants to dwell within it as His temple. As my thinking about myself becomes renewed, I can choose to take care of myself physically as well as emotionally, mentally and so on. As I look at Jesus, I do not see Him treating His body badly. He lives with a rhythm of rest and physical activity; He both disciplines and cares for Himself physically. Like Jesus, taking care of my body is taking care of the vehicle of the *message*, ensuring I am literally fit to do my part. I love God with all my body each time I lovingly steward the fleshly resource that He has provided for me.

But God also intends something deeper – that I love Him not half-heartedly but with an inner force that is unshakeable and will not be veered from its target. Again I must look to Jesus as my model:

Let us fix our eyes on Jesus, the author and perfecter of our faith, who for the joy set before him endured the cross, scorning its shame, and sat down at the right hand of the throne of God. Consider him who endured such opposition from sinful men, so that you will not grow weary or lose heart.

(Heb 12:2–3)

Where did His strength come from? Jesus was motivated by a future joy. There was something more that He was hoping for. What? The joy that was set before Him, the something more that He was hoping for was you. It was me. It was being face to face with us for ever in the presence of the Father. Now I can make neither head nor tail of this unless I consider two particular moments in my life when I would have literally moved mountains for the joy of seeing someone else face to face. Every mother who has gone through natural childbirth knows those moments. The energy expended and the desperation felt by myself as a woman in labour (particularly my first) is like no other work that a human being has to face.

Like every other woman in labour, I was literally faced with one of three options: my own death, the death of a beloved child as yet unseen, or a work of painful endurance requiring an inner strength that I never knew I possessed. They say that when a life is endangered, human beings will do incredible things to save and rescue that life. Amazing feats of strength appear from nowhere. The labour of childbirth is a lot like that. And it is not just the desire for my own life or the life of my child that drove me as a mother, but it was principally the imminent joy of being face to face with that baby. Twice now in my lifetime, that joy set before me kept me pushing in pain for hours on end. On each occasion I longed to see my baby with an inner might that would brook no opposition.

Many years down the road, I can still feel my strong longing for my children. Even as they enter adult life, I find myself fascinated by the people they are becoming. I deeply long to see them face to face as adults and in many ways I find myself still 'pushing' with all my might! This is simply what it means to be a healthy adult woman: to biologically long for your potential or actual children and so realise the incredible strength necessary to selflessly love, whether or not that biological urge is fulfilled.

As I think about it, I see this is similar to the way my husband loves me as his wife. He seems to experience a similarly strong biological urge to be intimately face to face with me, as lover to beloved. Again and again he expresses this through his willingness to selflessly sacrifice himself in order to bless me as the object of his desire. (Even as I write he is busy doing the household chores in order that I do not have to do them later.) This is simply what it means to be a healthy adult man: to biologically long for your potential or actual wife and so realise the incredible strength necessary to offer an enduring, selfless love, whether or not that biological urge is fulfilled. I guess that puts the difficulty that a man experiences in selflessly loving his wife on a par with a woman's suffering in childbirth, and the painful sacrifice of healthy masculine celibacy on a par with the ache that comes to a woman's heart through childlessness. Thinking of it this way really helps me understand and empathise with the opposite gender! Whether male or female, when I am aiming to love God, I need the same desire, the same inner might that will topple every idol that stands in the way of the one true God. But do I want to be face to face with God that much?

What would I do? Mostly I fix my eyes on what is seen – the difficulty of the journey – rather than the unseen joy of intimacy with God. So I usually give up almost as soon as I have begun. How can I change?

What would Jesus do? I need to take Jesus' strength as my own day after day for, in truth, I have none of my own. Jesus is the one who has both tried and succeeded. He has already gone though the labour to end all labours so that we will eventually meet face to face, adult to adult. Jesus is the one continuing century after century, wooing us all towards intimacy as our lover.

If Jesus is the hero to top all heroes then in each of my relationships, in each interaction, I need be His local hero, representing Him, communicating His love in every way. To do this I need to fix my eyes on Jesus, to literally put Jesus between myself and the other person:

me   Jesus   you

Jesus is my defence and my shield, absorbing the impact of your sins against me. He clothes my nakedness and provides for me in my need. And, in reality, it is to Him that I offer myself as I seek to bless you. As I fix my eyes on Him, and love Him with all my heart and with all my soul and with all my mind and with all my strength, I simply need to do the next thing He wants me to do with you, my neighbour. And what might that be? He may ask me to selflessly give to you or He may ask me to warmly receive from you. For me, whether you are male or female or whether I am giving or receiving will need to make no difference. For the joy set before me of seeing you face to face, rather than mask to mask, I simply need to communicate the *message*, laying my life down for Him and therefore for you, as I am willing to be His local hero:

As the Father has loved me, so have I loved you. Now remain in my love... My command is this: Love each other as I have loved you. Greater love has no one than this that he lay down his life for his friends. You are my friends if you do what I command... This is my command: Love each other.

(Jn 15:9, 12–14, 17)

The road to real freedom

However, just as with the exodus of the Israelites from Egypt and the persecution of the infant Church, very rapidly I find that the freedom I choose in relationships is put to the test. One minute I think that I have changed for good when I have managed just once to love someone well enough. Choosing to offer a simple and more or less selfless action in the life of another human being brings me such joy! No longer bound under the rule of self-centred autonomy, when my will is even temporarily submitted to almighty God I feel the ecstasy of the freedom of finally being His. All seems right with the world.

But the next minute that person reacts to my love in a way that seems, from my perspective, to rubbish the very treasure I have so selflessly offered. Good has been repaid with evil. Love has been repaid with hatred. What will I do? I might want to go away and sulk, thinking anxious or angry or shame-based thoughts, wishing I had never been so noble. Selfless vulnerability could be so rapidly replaced by selfish self-protection. The ecstasy of freedom tends to evaporate as the pain of personal rejection or worthlessness or inadequacy sets in. If I am still willing to listen to the Holy Spirit, usually it will gradually dawn on me that I am called to love irrespective of the reception. God calls me to keep on going on towards Christ-likeness, but it seems beyond me. The fallen structure of my heart that drags me back to seek the comfort of my relational style seems far too powerful.

At this point, I identify strongly with my brothers and sisters, the Israelite nation after the exodus, facing a seemingly uncrossable sea, the boundary between Egypt and the desert route towards their true home in the promised land. For myself in relationships, the boundary is the choice between selfishness and the possibility of selflessness, independence and the beginnings of dependence, remaining in darkness and walking in the light, relating with a mask and finding a route to true intimacy with God and with others.

Like the Israelites, I find myself standing on the Egyptian side of the Sea of Reeds, not yet letting the water lap at my toes. I look towards the other side, the Sinai Peninsula. It is the road to real freedom. The terrain is definitely harsher over there. Outside the protection of my relational style, I will be vulnerable in a fallen world. I know how to get by in Egypt and I do not know much about Sinai. I can dig water channels from the Nile to feed myself daily, and I do not know how to walk into an endless desert and simply trust that God will provide. I know how to protect myself amid the Fall and I do not know much about Christ.

As I look towards Sinai, at my back stands the army from hell. My own independent flesh, the world and the devil have woken up to the battle at hand. Collectively, their presence seems far too intimidating and powerful. Before me is the call of God that I am finally hearing, but it seems impossible to follow. Behind me the enemy holds weapons against me. I consider the pain I may feel in vulnerably obeying God. People I try to love will almost certainly repay me with evil as well as good. I am trapped. Like the Israelites, I cry: *'Was it because there were no graves in Egypt that you brought us to the desert to die?... It would have been better for us to serve the Egyptians than to die in the desert'* (Ex 14:11–12).

What is the *message* that I need to hear? *'Do not be afraid. Stand firm and you will see the deliverance the Lord will bring you today. The Egyptians you see today you will never see again. The Lord will fight for you; you need only to be still'* (Ex 14:13–14).

In whatever area of my relational style where I am doing battle, the bottom line is that the battle belongs to God not me. I have no power to defeat the fall within me; He has. I need only to be still and depend completely upon Him, even in the midst of the threat of pain and apparent defeat. It is the same *message* it has always been. I am His child, I am His beloved, I am the temple of His Spirit.

Then what? As with the Israelites, God seeks to develop my faith in Him as my redeemer. He will open up a way for me to respond rightly, to cross the sea as if on dry land and get to the other side. And those particular Egyptians (my flesh, the world and the devil) I will never see again. He will bring change in my life. But it will challenge my faith just as it did with the Israelites. In practice this means a testing process where this particular part of my relational style can be left behind for ever and I can, in that area of my relationships, begin to develop towards Christ-likeness.

Let me give you an example. I have mentioned how my relational style with a few women could be emotionally dependent, and even sexualised. I started working with God on this area of my relational style over fifteen years ago. Since then, God has been inviting me to dependently cross the 'sea of reeds' while He has been doing battle on my behalf with that particular enemy stacked against me. My job was to fix my eyes on Him and choose dependent trust. His job was to direct my path and defeat the enemy behind me. In that time, I have walked across the somewhat terrifying and difficult 'dry ground' of personal change with the towering walls of water to my right and to my left and the taunts of the enemy in my ears: *'You'll never change. The world and half the Church says that you're OK as you are. Quit God and come back and get your life from "Woman" instead of Him.'*

Or perhaps in later years: *'The Church will never believe that you're different. They'll never give you the benefit of the doubt. Once a sinner, always a sinner. They'll never let you minister again. You're finished as a Christian. Give up!'*

I see that for many years now, I have been standing vulnerably on the opposite bank, the coarse sand of 'Sinai'. As I have looked back towards 'Egypt', there has been nothing to see. The enemy is long dead. The waves that had parted to allow me to cross have systematically drowned that particular army that was set against me. By the grace of God, I will never see them again, and, wonderfully, I am changed for ever.

But that does not mean that there are not other armies, other aspects of 'Egypt' from which God seeks to free me. Every day, the

Holy Spirit helps me to see that in different areas of my heart, I am still stuck in Egypt and still very much in need of His loving deliverance. Throughout my days as a fallen disciple of Christ, I will need to tread that weary path from cross to garden tomb, between the Nile delta and the sand of Sinai, learning to die to self and be raised with Him as a new creation.

But as I take that journey, I can rejoice. I have begun to grasp how wide and long and high and deep is the love of Christ both for me and His Church. I have seen with my own eyes the great power that He displays against the simple evil of fallen creatures (both my own flesh, the world and the devil). The more I see Him display that power, the more I witness and experience the wonderful and complex good that He weaves, and the more I fear Him and put my trust in Him alone. The more I trust Him, the easier it becomes to walk the long discipleship road, because the more I come to love Him in return:

> *'Because he loves me,' says the LORD, 'I will rescue him; I will protect him, for he acknowledges my name. He will call upon me, and I will answer him; I will be with him in trouble, I will deliver him and honour him. With long life will I satisfy him and show him my salvation.'*
>
> (Ps 91:14–16)

APPENDIX

One step on the road towards fulfilling the high calling of Jesus' prayer in John 17 would be to create a short course for Christians offering practical help, teaching and skills in basic relationship issues and exploring God's fundamental design for community, based upon the Trinity. Hence *Get Real!*

Over the last few years, Community Church, Southampton has seen many hundreds of people attending the discipleship course *Get Real!* which is now available for use in other pastoral contexts. The course offers creative teaching (including role play and testimony), individual, pair and facilitated group work, and forges structured links with the local church pastoral team. Using a mix of compassion and challenge, we aim to provide a varied 'tool-box' environment through which both God and His people can effectively communicate and relate. Without attempting to provide solutions or focused therapy, *Get Real!* seeks to disrupt our self-centred style of relating with others and to draw us towards intimate dependence on God and healthy interdependence with our neighbour.

 *'Get Real in Relationships – The Message'* is a one day event offering a brief introduction to some of the basic concepts and methods of the full course:

Calling – exploring how true fellowship in Christian community effectively communicates the gospel message of reconciliation.

Communicating – what underlying message are we *actually* communicating through the way we typically relate?

Connecting – examining the roots of our current way of relating, making connections with past experience.

Changing – exploring what we really think of God, allowing Him to draw us towards change.

Christ – encouraging the renewal of our thinking and bold Christ-like love in relationship.

The taster day varies in presentation depending upon the needs of the venue, but usually includes creative teaching, testimony, the Lord's Supper and facilitated small group work. Group facilitators can be provided through Cornerstone Network. The aim is to give the flavour of the full course, while still briefly offering the concepts in a useable format for those attending.

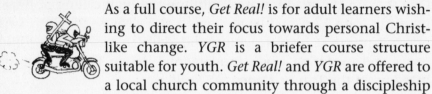

As a full course, *Get Real!* is for adult learners wishing to direct their focus towards personal Christ-like change. *YGR* is a briefer course structure suitable for youth. *Get Real!* and *YGR* are offered to a local church community through a discipleship process. This usually begins by inviting us to run our taster day in your area. Following that, for at least two full courses, we aim to walk alongside you, teaching and enabling your local team before inviting you to run the course under licence.

A typical *Get Real!* team consists of two or three co-ordinators and a number of group facilitators, who together make up about a quarter of the total course membership. Team members will typically be pastorally gifted and established in a local church. To help disciple a local team, we initially provide one course co-ordinator, teaching staff and half of the group facilitators. We also offer pre-course training, feedback and debriefing for all team members. We ask that you provide a suitable venue, local pastoral co-ordinators and the remaining group facilitators. Ideally, the adult course runs for twelve sessions either weekly or over several weekends.

Further information about running a *Get Real!* course under licence from Cornerstone Network can be obtained from:

Get Real!, Community Church, Central Hall, St Mary Street, Southampton, SO14 1NF, UK. Tel. +44 (0) 23 8073 7710. email: info@getrealcourse.org   website: www.getrealcourse.org

Further copies of this book can be purchased from Matteh Publications at the same address.

Get Real! uses concepts from the adapted Crabb/CWR counselling model as presented and taught by Central Counselling and Training Service, Southampton. Further information about training courses for pastoral workers, counsellors and counselling supervisors who wish to use this counselling model can be obtained from Central Counselling and Training Service by phoning +44 (0) 23 8023 7230, or emailing normaparrack@cornerstone-network.org

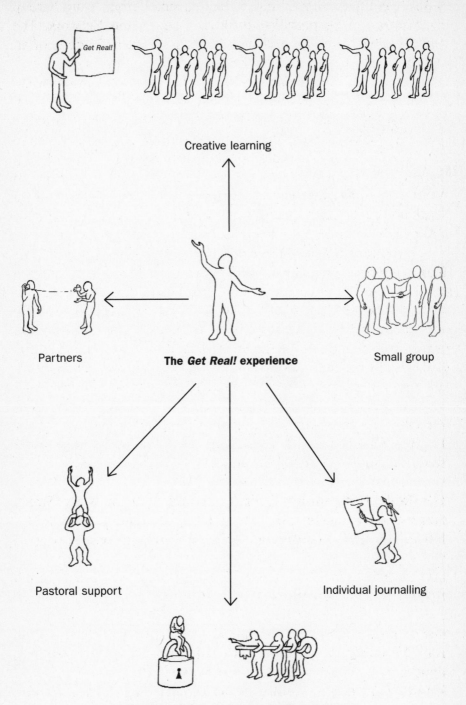

Creative learning

Partners

The *Get Real!* experience

Small group

Pastoral support

Individual journalling

(Facilitators only) Training, feedback and debrief

BIBLIOGRAPHY

Atkinson, D., *The Message of Genesis 1–11* (BST, IVP 1990).

Augsburger, D., *Caring Enough to Confront* (Regal Books, 1981).

Berkof, L., *Systematic Theology* (Banner of Truth, 1958).

Bonhoeffer, D. (Weber, M., ed.; Scott, D., trans.), *Meditations on the Cross* (Westminster John Knox Press, 1998).

Broughton Knox, D., *The Everlasting God* (Evangelical Press, 1982).

Crabb, L., *Inside Out* (NavPress, 1988).

Crabb, L., *Finding God* (Zondervan, 1994).

Douglas, J.D., et al., *New Bible Dictionary* (IVP, 1982).

Dryden, W. and Yankura, J., *Developing Rational Emotive Behavioural Counselling* (Sage, 1995).

Dryden, W., *Preparing for Client Change in Rational Emotive Behaviour Therapy* (Whurr Publications, 1995).

Ferguson, S.B., Wright, D.F., eds, Packer, J.I., consulting ed., *New Dictionary of Theology* (IVP, 1988).

Janov, A., *The New Primal Scream* (Abacus, 1990).

Johnson, L.T., *The Writings of the New Testament* (SCM Press, 1986).

Lewis, C.S., *A Grief Observed* (Faber & Faber, 1961); *Letters to Malcolm: Chiefly on Prayer* (Fount, 1977); *The Problem of Pain* (Fount, 1998); *The Weight of Glory* (MacMillan, 1949).

Luther, M., *Second Commentary to the Seven Penitential Psalms* (quoted from Bonhoeffer, D., *op. cit.*).

Mehrabian, A., *Silent Messages* (Wadsworth, 1971).

Payne, L., *The Healing Presence* (Kingsway, 1990).

Peterson, E., *The Message* (Navpress, 1993).

Stott, J., *The Cross of Christ* (IVP, 1989).

Vine, W.E., *Expository Dictionary of Old and New Testament Words* (World Bible, 1981).

Williams, M., *The Original Velveteen Rabbit* (Mammoth, 1992 [first pub. 1922]).

Winnicott, D.W., *Maturation Processes and the Facilitating Environment* (Hogarth, 1965).

ENDNOTES

1. Williams, M., *The Original Velveteen Rabbit* (Reed Books, 1992; first pub. 1922), pp. 8–9.
2. Broughton Knox, D., *The Everlasting God* (Evangelical Press, 1982).
3. Atkinson, D., *The Message of Genesis 1–11* (BST, IVP, 1990).
4. Lewis, C.S., 'The Weight of Glory', *Screwtape Proposes a Toast* (Collins, 1965).
5. Luther, M., *Second Commentary to the Seven Penitential Psalms*, quoted in Bonhoeffer, D. (Weber, M., ed., Scott, D., trans.), *Meditations on the Cross* (Westminster John Knox Press, 1998).
6. John Stott, *The Cross of Christ* (IVP, 1989).
7. Morris, L.L., *New Dictionary of Theology* (IVP, 1988).
8. Bonhoeffer, D., *op. cit.*
9. Lewis, C.S., *Letters to Malcolm: Chiefly on Prayer* (Fount, 1977), p 83.
10. Chesterton, G.K., *What's Wrong with the World* (1910, pt. 1).
11. Johnston, L.T., *The Writings of the New Testament* (SCM Press, 1986).